Intimate Disclosures

Religion, Poetry, Sexuality, Illusion, Reality, and Pervading Nostalgia

Intimate Disclosures

Religion, Poetry, Sexuality, Illusion, Reality, and Pervading Nostalgia

Singing Icons

Lawrence W. Manglitz

Library of Congress Control Number:		2016919980
ISBN:	Hardcover	978-1-5245-6570-1
	Softcover	978-1-5245-6571-8
	eBook	978-1-5245-6572-5

Print information available on the last page.

Rev. date: 01/06/2017

To order additional copies of this book, contact:
Xlibris
1-888-795-4274
www.Xlibris.com
Orders@Xlibris.com
724670

Contents

IV. Epiphanies

V. The Erotic Incarnation

Commentary...85

VI. Two Poets

VII. Turkey

VIII. Spain

IX. War

X. Random Writings

Song of a Man Who Has Come Through

Not I, not I, but the wind that blows through me!
A fine wind is blowing the new direction of time.
If only I let it bear me, carry me, if only it carry me!
If only I am sensitive, subtle, oh, delicate, a winged gift!
If only, most lovely of all, I yield myself and am borrowed
By the fine, fine wind that takes its course through the chaos of the world
Like a fine, exquisite chisel, a wedge-blade inserted;
If only I am keen and hard like the sheer tip of a wedge
Driven by invisible blows,
The rock will split, we shall come at the wonder, we shall find the Hesperides.*

Oh, for the wonder that bubbles into my soul,
I would be a good fountain, a good well-head,
Would blur no whisper, spoil no expression.

What is the knocking?
What is the knocking at the door at night?
It is somebody wants to do us harm

No, no, it is the three strange angels.**
Admit them, admit them.

D. H. Lawrence

---

*   Hesperides (Greek mythology): The place young maidens guarded, where the trees bore apples of gold.

**   Michael, Gabriel, Raphael: good angels.

Introduction

The challenge for me writing this narrative poetry and prose is that much of it comes from a long time ago, about an even earlier time—a web of nostalgia. I have strived to be truthful in my remembrance of those single moments. As I put these remembrances, each of the small pieces in an order, I wanted to be attentive to what vision I was trying to construct. Sometimes I was very conscious of doing this; but most of the time, it seemed a flowing subconsciousness. Each detail made and altered the remembrance. The original event, person, geography, and the creative imagination shaped the final piece. And at the conclusion of the writing, the poem seemed to establish itself, with many attentive revisions.

Henri Bergson, the French philosopher, writes that we do not have the same impression of a person or event in our immediate time that we had in the original perception. Many years have passed, which are filled with thousands of new events and people, and those give a new perspective to the vision of the past.

The day I perceived them originally—plowing, sleeping in my bed, talking with me on a porch, in one photograph with them, one remembrance of drinking gin with them on their veranda in the Algarve, one glance at a young man the first day of my teaching in Turkey, one swim near Mersin, one moment on the SS *AKdeniz*—is one time in their lives. And of course, these were all different times in my life, now echoing seventy-seven years of time. The attempt to record this echo has sometimes seemed dangerous and tragic—the evolution and honest revelation of a private life. These are important impressions, quite accurate, from important moments of intense being, apart from ordinary consciousness of daily life—quiet epiphanies. I suppose that I have written about them because I wanted to remember them, to understand them. I would admit that a part of me would return to them.

There is not a great sense of vulnerability for me in sharing these memories. But they have sometimes wounded me in recollection. It is a part of memory and life itself. They return or are summoned to enrich an evolving consciousness.

My journey within an oppressive religion, especially during my childhood and youth, destroyed any freedom for me to be who I understood myself to be and to express my sexual desire. That time generated so much fear and shame, walking in the shadows, keeping my secrets, and missing great opportunities for love and the sensual joy of my body.

I have reckoned with the oppression of my childhood religion in part through the freedom given to me in the Episcopal tradition; all has given me a definite awareness of that person who I am. Christianity has always been with me. I resolve all dualities and an ultimate mystery into him I call cosmic Christ, far from the fearful, destructive, conservative understanding of my youth. Christianity has, as new understandings have emerged, remained, and become a refreshed part of my knowledge. I cannot escape God, and the manifestation in the incarnation of that deity in Christ, in the Christian religion—the bond which makes meaning of my life. Many would take issue with this resolution and peace of mind, considering that I am a gay man. It is my restructuring of the meanings of that incarnation that seem urgently needed to keep Christianity relevant to the enlightenment of current contemporary theology and the new knowledge of Western culture.

* * *

Without the encouragement and comments of many friends, straight and gay, the wise and compassionate Episcopal clergy who have shared their spirituality and listened with care to my journey, and the help I received formatting this book, this work would not exist. I express deep gratitude to all of them. And I give my thanks to all my students who have taught me. To the men I have loved and been loved by I would acknowledge that their intimacy with me has sustained the currents of my life and brought much joy and a sense of godliness, and the mysterious wonder and struggle of creation. This work would celebrate this.

I have a great sense of the support of my family and the knowledge, wisdom, and questions of my many teachers and professors who have been important in shaping my vision. I am grateful that I have escaped the oppression and hypocrisy in the history of the church and embraced the great teachings, icons, and rituals of religion, not because they are not of literal significance, but because they lead to the epiphanies that speak of our yearnings and a hope of fulfilling them: of granting equality to all and attempting to bring the joy of abundant life to all. But still in the name of Deity, we slaughter and bring to many more than those killed, a suffering and twisting of their created being and deprivation of existence that they endure all their lives.

Lawrence William Manglitz
January 5, 2016, Grand Rapids, Michigan

I

CHILDHOOD AND FAMILY SACREDNESS

Sweet Boy Alone, Spinning with Pegasus and the Holy Ghost: 1945 Bridgeman, Michigan

Far from his house, with collected birds' eggs, seed pods, and the blue feather;
in a field of tall dry grass, burned yellow, brittle, scratching,
was the merry-go-round: large, dangerous, a wild stallion to the boy.

In the distance, it stood idle, high above the earth,
an octagon of weathering wood and rusting metal,
brought all to a pleasure of new birth.

Inside the wood planks, a smooth iron bar, curved round,
a strong handle to hold, clutch hard against a force to throw a boy outward,
up to the air, and down to pounded ground;
a wide path circled the apocalyptic horse, a hundred children's feet, beating,
had run full speed pushing, then leaping onto the wood,
each grasped strong.

On two sides were the large pumping handles;
the wooden planks aged with splitting,
but no splinters existed; they had no chance to form;
the children's bodies and blood filled hands had worn all to shine:
gray wood and rusted iron.

At last, in dizzy motion, two boys in breathless madness jumped up;
one on each side of the spinning stallion,
pumped with strength the smooth steel to increase the speed,
creaking, moaning, loud grinding iron on iron,
lifting all the children to the swirling barn, distant lilacs in purple scent,
red apple orchard, gray wood house,
up to white clouds, and rush wind of May sky
and again, the speeding circle made the dancing blur,
as a painter's palette blending.

No one knew who built it, how long ago,
nor why it was in the middle of a field—
a nowhere place.

He, the solitary boy, would whirl himself,
spin: slow, faster, more,
until Pegasus lifted him to a distant space—
to moon, stars, a constellation,
his body and soul gasping, dazzled,
all muscles and nerves, in a storm of wind,
on that spinning divinity.

* * *

For the first time, late in life, I remember the remote field,
Marvel: joy and power there,
being one with all, the blended color.

I fear some building of houses
has made transcending disappear,
but in this moment, merriment rushes in, clamors clear;
this ecstasy claimed again,
cool wind breathing in my ear.

How the Baptist Church Almost Wrecked My Family: My Mother Dancing in the Movies: Selected Images from 1954

After Sunday dinner at the house of my grandmother and grandfather at 1751
Alto Street, the yellow house with the Judas tree in front, still there,
we were told to go to the backyard—
the summer garden of zinnias, asters, cosmos, and creeping vines;
the maple tree with autumn leaves flown later to Anatolia, in my grandmother's
letters,
out more to the place of the fish pond, with brown floating leaves in tainted water,
last winter's dead, to the bending willow, rustling out grief:
the first to be leafed and the last to lose.

Another home movie was about to be shot,
not quite a complete record of birthdays and holidays.
The history of my family between 1941 and 1969 exists today
in a black cassette box someplace in this house.

We went to the green yard, fresh scented,
nervous as if all the world would watch us walking around.
My grandfather held the camera aimed at us,
lined up, squinting: "Move to the right," and two of us lost our balance,
shuffling closer to the setting sun—slowly passing, the backyard always remaining;
and each of us immortal, I believed.

Beyond our daydreaming, the voice shouted, "It's on, do something, move."
We began our slow advance, waving, nodding,
as if the Romanovs in a black-and-white photograph that last day in St. Petersburg,
but for my brother turning summersaults. We lost our balance again.
Then a handkerchief falling, and through all the ages of our movie making,
my mother steps out of line and gracefully lifts her arms above her head;
so begins my mother's dancing.

The camera man turns away and follows her, as she extends delicately one leg,
dropping her arms slightly into an arch, lifting her head to the descending sun,
and with slow, soft ease begins to dance like a Parisian ballerina.
She glides, lifting her head to the West, laughing,
free from the sternness of the Baptist preacher, who spoke too often of sin and hell.
Now she bows, floating over to the hedge, turning, and quick light steps to the willow,
sometimes singing—it is her soul.
And in those moments as a young boy, I loved the magic of my mother, her grace,
her moments of happiness.

She never won at croquet. And would say things like
"Why do you always knock my ball into the hedge?
Are you going to send me into the fish pond? You are just a poopy!"
Dancing and singing were my mother's things,
dropping her mallet, she would waltz off to the sun,
beyond the pond, to distant fields,
twirling, twirling, in that long, perpetual summer of my youth,
her song echoing.

January 2009

Christmas in 1947

On Christmas Day, my father, mother, and brother
and I would drive up to my grandparents' house for dinner.
I would stay for three days.

Christmas Night, when the rest of the family would leave,
the coming of evening was a perfection;
my grandfather and grandmother were mine,
along with the house, and all outdoors.

Kneeling on the couch, I would gaze out the window
into a winter day grown dark:
the black lines of branches sharpened against the sodden gray sky,
above blue-white snow in dusk.

In my grandmother's plastic candle set, on the sill, were seven blue bulbs;
I could smell the heat of the glass, illuminating the world, their warm light
like a star sunning, or another Son borne into His own creation,
a new race rising.

The view out from the warmth and safety of the house,
        the never ending layers of a cold night,
        a vastness now muted to purple,
        bitter wind bleeding in through the glass,
        my breath a mist on the window,
        making the mystery,
        beyond the branches, the low hills,
        the distant railroad tracks,
        through to some infinity,
        a distant point, eternity,
        never seen,
        now downed over in falling flakes,
        white, but mostly cobalt,
was a silent certitude:
"Christ was born of Mary."

My grandmother would kiss me on my head: "Magic," she said,
looking toward the window,
while my grandfather smoked his rolled cigarettes in his chair,
lost always
in some distance—
the smoke curling up,
away.

No harm would come to us.
I was only a boy, a true believer, a child, spoiled by every wish granted,
not knowing the way of things—never dreaming of the drawing away of everything,
      not knowing that all:
      the blues lights,
      the house, the tree with three black crows,
      the canned peaches in the cellar,
      the fragrance of Windee Lotion, filling the house as my grandmother,
      after her bath, stood in her long night gown,
      in front of the hot register—an almond fragrance lifting,
      not knowing that all would be drawn out through the glass,
      beyond the sharp branches, tracks, hills,
      to the forever distance—
      eternity,
not knowing as a boy does not know.

In stillness, even this half century later,
      for scarce moments on Christmas Eve,
      when I am kneeling for the sacrament, or
      gazing at the layered branches of the evergreen,
      or standing on the porch in early night for air,
      staring out to the hazed moon,
it returns; all is drawn back,
      like the falling light of a spinning star,
      for marveling at the wonder of it,
      against all odds,
      making the mystery of Christmas come from far away:
      infinity's point of distance—
      this one more time, covering the night blue,
and for the moment, they return.

December 25, 2001

Thanksgiving Dinner in 1978

In Michigan, the long season of winter days
is a time when one day is seen in another the same:
gray turning to mysteries,
the enigmatic family,
the eventual long season of darkness;
a leaden gray mist hangs just above the corn stubble in black fields,
private sorrows and defeats, the family love,
holding them fractured,
each of us close to each, separated by religion
and the flaring, then fleeting moments of hatred, never held,
the giving up of ever being understood
and acceptance of understandings were not to be the factors,
but some other binding: our history together, and the known,
but seldom-spoken affection.

The childhood of my brother and me, stilled, not without the sweetness
of child's play: hide-and-seek in the dry fragrance of drying autumn leaves
until the streetlights came on,
the cotton-scented comfort of my mother's arms,
my father helping to make the perfect kite from yesterday's newspapers—
how straight it rose into the sky, skeleton branches reaching for the swaying tail
made from an old apron.

On Thanksgiving Day, my arrival at the back door, opened by my father, allowed
the escape of a steam cloud and the pungent fragrance of the dinner:
roasting meat: pork, chicken; and the bread dressing: sage, pork sausage, celery,
onion, pecans, and apples, a moisture of perfection, browned,
heavy crust, steam rising.

The two of them worked for hours in the making; my mother saying, "That isn't where
that knife goes, Wilbur. You'd better get the potato masher out. What did you do
with the gravy spoons? It is almost time."
And so with my mother's promptings and my father's patience,
the dinner was turned to a feast.

This they did for us; there were no other guests.
It was as if they had lifted the host at Eucharist;
they gave this dinner,
an emblem of more.

My father would lean part way out, holding open the storm door,
my mother just behind, excited like a child, contained within—they had been
waiting, nervously checking the time and doneness of the meats.

And when we would leave to go home; it was the same,
only my mother leaning out, my father behind.
I have seen photographs of them waving in cold December,
my mother clutching her sweater up to her neck.
And in the first days of spring and Easter, again.

* * *

After dinner my father, brother, and I would walk out in back of the house
to the long field, down to where my brother, as a child,
in hopes of great fortune to be harvested from trees,
planted a hundred pines.
"Let's walk out and look at the trees," a voice said.

My father mowed a path through what was a field wild with what grows in
unattended fields in Michigan. The mowed path was green grass winding among
velvet sumac, blackberries, shriveling Queen Anne's lace, milkweed, and thistle
seed pods to be removed from socks and cuffs back in the house.

The three of us were the only people to walk on that path—and just once a year,
like the ancient priest entering the Holy of Holies, the three men in my family
walked out to a small woods of pine, twenty-seven trees twisted too much by the
wind, disfigured, scrawny, and one of us would say, "It looks like a fortune."
It was a joke, but a shrine to the early ambitions and desires of my brother.

Eventually, most of the trees were bulldozed out for a subdivision,
others remained at precarious angles, a few still stood to make shade
for the backyards of suburban houses.

Another year had passed; we had walked his mown path.
Going back to the house, to see the rusted barrel where once our hound
had slept, a chicken killer,
his lead fastened to a long wire that allowed him running, but now no longer
endangering our neighbors chickens,
which he had several times brought home, half dead.
My father would say, "Bury that chicken—bury that chicken before they see."
But I would say, "It isn't dead yet."
Once a white hen, red blood spattered
carefully laid to rest by me
was suddenly resurrected from her grave, all on her own—
wings and blood,
flapping, flinging—terror;
the chicken and I ran to our separate safety.

And then in that November wind, when my father, brother, and I returned,
we passed one of the windows in the living room;
my mother was holding up my youngest niece,
Sharla Jean, to the glass.
"Wave to your uncle," only the lips moving.

My mother was happy with all this family about her, and my father.
We were all mellowed out to peace, with stretching ease,
in late afternoon gray.
And I thought: now time stop.
All be safe from death,
let this remain. This one moment in time
with an abundance of Thanksgiving dinner,
my brother and I walking together, which we seldom do,
and my father proud to have his sons beside him walking on his path
on the path mowed all the summer long for these few times that we walked together
in silence, almost total silence:
the autumn pilgrimage to the past and foiled dreams,
but contented in the present time.

I know now it was my father who watched year by year the growth of the pines,
His own garden like his strength to be, smaller vines of squash and tomatoes.
It was my father who, mowing the grass, dreamed our return.

It amazes me so strange a thing. Why did he do it?
And amazing, I never asked.
But then perhaps the mowing did not seem strange in my father's fields.

I knew that in approaching day, it would be
our putting away of each other,
one by one—I was right.

Then how silently we would stand.

How incomprehensible that all our Thanksgiving dinners had finished, vanished.
And sixty billion years ahead for earth before the sun would dim—eternal time
for earth would be minus our silent pilgrimages—journeys, so full in a silence,
consuming each other's souls, we thought our deepest thoughts,
saw our love for each had trapped each for each;
we could never free ourselves.

Great Aunt Bess in Soft Colors

She sat within the shadow of the lampshade,
the embroidery frame and white cloth stretched flat in the direct light,
her partially illumined face, like a mask,
the light catching the strong lenses of the wired framed glasses like small slivers
of ice,
the face bent down to the fabric, as she pulled the hues of yellow, blue, and pink
threads into shapes of leaves, petals, baskets of flowers,
and singing canary birds
on pillow cases, dresser scarves, dish towels: her Christmas gifts.
This weaving, at night, replacing the drab of the day.

It was in the fabric and colors she lived,

Bess, whose husband Jack fell from a roof to his death,
became one of the impoverished ones
who lived with my grandmother Kate,
in the big house. She was a short woman with short hair too.
During the day, she folded boxes at the Grand Rapids Box Board Company in
Grandville.
When the day ended, she took a bus from her work to downtown and shopped for
vases, colored threads, and the white fabric with printed blue patterns to follow
with a needle from Woolworth's.

Then with her transfer, she took the Madison bus to Franklin Street and the house
painted "battle ship gray." My grandmother, Kate, said, "With black trim."
The vases held the pink roses from the wire fence at 811 Major Place Court,
still there until three years ago, when it was leveled to make an asphalt parking lot.
It was the rose bush I always wanted to see when I drove my old Impala through
the court, the rubber tires snapping twigs and small branches, the irregular beat
of a clock.

Each Easter, I include her name in the church program for those for whom the white
lilies, yellow tulips, blue hyacinths, and pink roses are given: *Bessie Rypma;*
she was buried in 1954—the flower colors soft from the stained glass windows, as
if sewn by her on white cotton.

No one in the church ever heard of her.
But when I see her name, I see an ancient woman weaving
in the dim light of a falling day; sometimes smoking Old Gold cigarettes, the blue
smoke curling and wisping in the slender beams of light coming through grape vines
that surrounded the house and all of us inside, safe pilgrims in the dusk
at 811 Major Place Court, as if in the chancel of some great church,
where blue incense pungent in a Far Eastern aroma vanishes to darkness.

And she sits far away, a China doll, her feet not touching the floor,
pulling silk thread through fabrics that for years held safely sleeping heads.

2011

Two Remembrances of My Father

Remembrance One

Tonight I am haunted by my father's short dying;
his hands above the clean white sheet,
which he smoothed and neatly folded and unfolded—hem-like:
a sacred task—this making of his pall,
this cocking of his head, birdlike;
he stared with one good eye at the evenness of his shroud.

Later, his hands fluttered above the white sheets:
arranging, picking up, and putting down in another place
the nuts, bolts, washers, screws, nails in his tool box, he explained,
imposing order on the chaos to the end of making things;
suddenly shouting east is east, west is west, north is north, south is south,
making firm the tenants of his faith;
or just holding on to what was left of reality.

When after his death and all he had was dismantled, moved out too quickly,
I took those things from his tool box: nails and bolts,
and the visions too, like verses from the book of Revelation,
blood flowing as high as the horses' bridles.

For years as a child, I had lived in the fear of the Second Coming of Christ,
waking in the middle of the night to the silence of the house,
remembering the warning: "Two shall be in the field; one taken, the other left."
The dancing shadows of winter branches and the streetlight gone wild in fear;
and I knew that all were gone—only one was left.
At fifty-four, I had to forgive the terror given to me.
Christ in light beyond death and the grave.
All creation waiting for that rising of the dead in Christ first;
then the living caught up; it would happen in the twinkling of an eye.

We could never agree on the meaning of these things.
And I have not been able to remove the claws.

I placed the bolts and nails on a shelf in my bedroom,
beneath the crucifix from Palma Majorca.
along with a collection of shells from Ibiza,
a rock from the wall in the Talas garden,
pieces of glass worn centuries smooth
in the relentless motion of the sea,
and one long blue jay feather, marked with black and white.
Above all these, the Holy Spirit hovered,
wings beating mystery after mystery, now revealed to my father and mother,
"face to face beheld."

How quiet he was in his dying, never speaking, awed to the largeness of the event
except for one night; he talked to the nurse's aide until morning,
telling her stories, laughing; she told us later.
It must be some drug removed his reserve
or our absence made him at ease;
and he unfolded his history to this thin, knitting stranger,
but to us, no word spoken, nothing,
nor did he ever speak of his childhood, or the days with his family;

All loveliness of childhood, his courting my mother,
hunting with his father near Baldwin;
the stories not spoken, were forever locked
under the heavy lid of his rose terra-cotta vault;
and we buried a man I never knew.

* * *

Remembrance Two

My father,
now dead ten years,
raised tomatoes, corn, squash, cucumbers, and peppers.
It is the tomatoes I most remember—
my looking at the young green plants,
some allowed to lay along the earth,
others he fastened up,
tying them with pieces
of shredded white sheets to wooden stakes.
About the base of each plant, a double strip of newspaper,
like a small wall—"to protect against the cut worms."

It is the tomatoes that now I taste most, brought in for our dinner,
with pork chops and corn:
"just picked fresh from the garden,"
we said those words each time—
a liturgical response.

Some summers we had too much rain, some not enough,
and some the pheasants pecked holes through the tight, red skin,
but the good summers provided us plenty, enough for canning
and to give away,
enough even for some rotting on the ground
in late September.

Each day he walked out to the garden;
returning to the house, he spoke
the progress or the harm.

It seems little I ever did for my father;
only once watering his plants
when he was in the hospital;
dragging the long black hose
across the parching grass
to where the branches of the plants bent down with the clusters
of green and dawning red tomatoes.

Time has moved so much away;
they, the tomatoes, our green house, and the barking dog gone too;
and the elm trees, burning bush, wild blackberries are vanished—
irrevocable in God's design.

I dream now out to the field to eat the warm redness,
the juices running down my chin.

I would ask him what he said that last night,
to lighten the mystery
of his life and dying,
this silent priest
of rich, dark earth.

Dying in the Morning Scent of Huckleberries

The scent of huckleberries drifted out in my father's dying breath.
He seldom spoke from his white bed—only complained of a ceiling needing paint:
"That ceiling has to get painted," he said as he moved his head up and around.

Mostly he folded the hem on his sheet, over again into wrinkles,
drawing the fabric to himself;
then smoothed all away, to begin again.

Today I don't know if he felt any sorrow, any regrets about his marriage,
the curtailed work on the railroad, or his sons far from him in religion;
he had stopped speaking of the book of Daniel
and the missionary conferences at the Baptist church—it was all of life for him.
His sons would hear nothing of it. And the arguments . . .

Now in that bleached room silence wiped out all time;
and the scent of huckleberries rose on his breath,
offered like an incense rising,
cleansed all hatred away . . .
what had been sharp, was filed down.

I stared out the window to the roofs of downtown houses
and concluded little we knew of each other's lives:
the other's meanings made to live,
dared not share our greatest fear
or ecstasy—
to speak it out, for fear of a knife
to cut.

In the sound of the drawing out and drawing in of breath,
were memories of our childhood:
recollections of a grassy slope,
and the cottage on Peacock Lake,
where his mother and I, a child, picked huckleberries, as he in his own childhood.
Each blue roundness sounding, hitting the bottom of the pail.

Once my grandmother rolled down the hill,
a large cotton ball of apron, stockings, pink petticoat, blue cotton dress,
over and over, then not a scratch, standing again.
We laughed a stomachache.
She told me that fifty-five years ago, the old man in the cottage next door
was stung by bumble bees—twenty-seven stings; he almost died.
Did bees live among the huckleberries?
Not in that early morning of summer 1943.
The sun was on my arms while I ate.
I could not name the warm succulence
beneath my tongue in the fading summer of innocence.

I told my father it was a lovely memory for me.
Startled, he looked at me, as if to understand some mystery, some large confusion.

"She picked blackberries for pies; it must have been blackberries."
        "Huckleberries," I said. "I remember the smallness."

And we fell into a deep silence, stretching back to those days when a herd of cows
meandered slowly down across the bridge; their bells ringing
in the dusk, I had never heard before,
and now again in this white room I feel the comfort of the slow gait,
the rhythmic swaying of the animals,
vanishing into their dust.

This dreaming out returns the tin cup, dappled blue and white
and pump, where I could prime and coax the water up,
with the clanging of the handle, loose.
The iron handle wobbling in the sucking up of air,
then gush,
like a mountain stream.
The cup was chipped, and when I tipped it to my lips,
the cold water ran down my naked belly—in a gasp, I laughed;
the ice taking my breath away.

And then in his green boat, his father fishing for bass:
I was not to move and did not, but stared at the green-purple dragon flies,
suspended, then darting away.

Now next to my father's bed, I fell lost into what was summoned up from that place
in childhood where there was no electricity
and my grandmother baked pies in an oven, fired with burning wood.
The juices bubbled, a perfection of rivulets from fork marks in the crust.

Thus, I stood beside him, that silent man, his life a mystery;
so much lost in small argument. I was afraid to speak.
What words were to be spoken, anyway, but to say, "I remember your family
father, Kate and William, and Bessie doing embroidery work in the corner, dresser
scarves and pillow cases made for Christmas—she worked every night for years,
with silk, shining threads of lightest yellow, green, and pink.
The needle flew beneath a leaden elephant incense burner on the window sill, next
to the ruby glass, Ottawa Beach engraved on the side.
She had, in all her days, traveled twenty-seven miles;
and the green boat your father made for me.
And your mother letting me have Aunt Bessie's wedding ring.

"Maybe they were blackberries after all.
As I think back, it seems so."

He said, "Yes, she picked blackberries near the woods, for pies."

And silence for a moment placed us on the sun slope of tall grass;
he seemed at peace with the words made right,
and for a time, a boy again, with his mother.

We each saw berries among tall ferns shine in morning light: purple, black;
a mystery created: these visions returning in breathing out the scent of berries;
some word he whispered for a moment in the air, dispersed.

2010

A Christmas Vision in 1953

At night, when I would stay with my grandfather and grandmother
during my winter vacation, after my bedtime treat of a black cow,
I would be sleepy on the sofa;
my grandfather, finished reading stories to me,
would go to the piano in the dining room
and play, improvising, "Some Day My Prince Will Come."

My grandmother would emerge from the bathroom after her bath,
wearing her long cotton night gown and soft blue robe.
She would have covered her body with an almond lotion: *Windee*.
Rubbing her hands, she would stand in front of the register,
while the rising heat would fill her gown; and the fragrance of almond
drifted to corners in the room.

The sound of the piano and her scent would blend—
always into a comfortable love and sadness,

My eyes would open and close on the shinning Christmas tree,
until I was scooped up and carried to my bed,
to the coolness of the silk eider down,
my toes reaching for the warmth of the hot water bottle.

"The Prince is Christ," my grandfather said.
He had his mythology.

I knew it was Leif, the boy who lived next door.
And going to sleep, I fell through the night to him,
my companion who knew the way through Dunn's Woods.

He would come someday.

March 5, 2001

811 Major Place Court SE

My Grandmother Kate:

She outlived almost everyone—
two husbands:
Floyd Thurber, who ran off with another woman;
and William, who fished at the cottage in a green flat bottomed boat;
her sister, Bessie, who sat after dinner in a chair,
at the foot of the steps,
a floor lamp with a faded shade of a great ship with all sails full in the wind—the
light coming just over her shoulder to her lap,
embroidered,
with pink, light green, blue,
and creamy yellow threads,
each night of the year, pillow cases, dresser scarves,
and fine handkerchiefs;
or she read children's books: *Bob Chester's Grit, Black Beauty,*
Trixie Beldon and the Secret of the Green Mansion, Bob Son of Battle;
Toby Tyler Joins the Circus.
all of which she gave to great nephews and nieces;
and the embroidered cotton
and linen she wrapped in crinkling paper,
for the wives of her nephews nieces, who did little in return.
She lived in a perpetual state of Christmas,
taking breaks to smoke an Old Gold cigarette, too quickly,
light blue smoke curling like clouds above the sailing ship;
she was the only woman in the family who swore;
and she was the only person who laughed
after that fateful Thanksgiving dinner,
when I told my story about the woman whose ass caught fire on a bus—or so the
bus driver thought. I still remember the gasps.

Kate's favorite son, Floyd, who, after he married, killed himself,
whose name she only mentioned twice;
Frist, when I was a kid, sixteen, wanting always to drive, asked where she wanted
to go.
She said to see Floyd's grave at Woodlawn Cemetery. We went and found the
grave, the moss and grass almost covering the stone.
He died in 1936, two years before I was born, falling away in time.
My thinking blurred with no comprehension;

And then again, when I was in college, when she was slowly losing her mind,
she suddenly had leaned forward to me in her rocking chair
and said we brought Floyd home;
and when they carried his coffin into the house
at 811 Major Place Court SE, it was covered with sleet.
a fact I could not comprehend.
The fact blurred into her pain.
I remembered the tombstone
almost covered with the spreading grass of years.

Ever since the time of his death,
making it difficult for us to find the grave,
wandering around and she with bad knees,
lurching on the steep hill among the single graves,
mostly of children.

The Next-Door Neighbor Maude:

Among lilacs and iris,
beneath the dark primal shade
of the catalpa tree
and my grandfather's arbor of grape vines,
which danced shadows on the dining room floor
where I had sat, turning the pages of old magazines:
The National Geographic opened a world of generous lust,
while I turned the pages,
gazing on the handsome men of Africa;
"They go naked,"
the child thought.
The men lined up to seventeen in a row,
with spears in their hands;
and the child with the magnifying glass in his hand
gazed on the strange, little *dickies*.
I watched Maude Samine,
sitting on a painted blue kitchen chair,
combing her long hair, which fell to the earth,
lost in tall grass and weeds,
her seven cats about her in the sun.

* * *

My brother and I lurking in the bushes,
once breathed out the words,
"She is a witch,
look at that black cat."
She sat in the white sun, drying, combing, brushing her white hair,
her seven cats
weaving in and out
between her legs
and the legs of the chair,
disturbing small insects
among the blue iris
as tall as we who crouched,
our knees down into the
green, dew grass and wet earth,
holding our breath,
hearing the
primal "coo, coo,"
she sang to her cats,
in early morning.

She lived in the smallest house, alone,
for years, even after my grandmother died.

1990

Avoiding the Empty Bed on a Rainy Night in January

I. A Game of Two-Handed Hearts

Fatigue slumbers on his lids, tearing the eyes.
He had won this night the last game of cards,
with only two pages of *The Night Train to Lisbon* remaining,
for later reading, in that narrow grave chamber;
but ashamed to admit he thought the winning important victory—solitary,
a late night ritual to still chaos.
Who would know his ritual, compulsive pleasure, after all,
his game to put off the empty bed,
this secret in his nights—
passing the moments before some obscure ending,
before reclining on white sheets:
a cold vault.

However, a game lost would have darkened the night more.
The book would be finished, a momentary delving into revolution
and the end of life: Amadeu de Prado's and his own:
some vessel in the brain erupting in the moonlight,
catching unawares, not known to the dying.

He could not stop without the comfort of tricking this game,
destined a paltry nothing,
done heartless by a card playing machine,
putting the king of spades
in someone else's yard.

* * *

Gazing out the spattered library window,
with no other prompt than his reflected face, distorted, childlike,
in running drops of rain, down, down the glass,
his mind swung into Rena Street, to his grandfather and grandmother's house;
she would be there weed pulling.
It was the Eden of no meaning, just being
in oak shadows and scattered petals after rain—

Heading north on this street drifting back from the 1940s Rena,
then the house last seen seventy years ago.
tonight he imagines the fern garden gone, the lilacs, the lazy sprinkler vanished.
Stalbergs next door dead certainly by now;
these vagaries creeping back.

What made the place return this winter night:
a remembrance of a 1943 Pontiac,
the tires cold humming on wet pavement,
like a smeared mirror reflecting back the irretrievable?

Each day since boyhood, that summer was distancing the pathway
to games in early Eden: a catalpa tree cut down;
the sound of his grandfather
playing the piano and cussing, smoking his rolled cigarette,
flicking ashes in the green glass tray,
smoke like incense, a blue wisp raised
now ceased these seventy years ago;
and dust settling down over the jewels in a broach, dropped on the hard floor
a half century ago or more.

She had worn it once on her violet dress, lace about the neck;
dressing in the bright bathroom light;
the boy knew beneath was her pink corset and brassiere;
the old woman whirled out the scent of *Evening in Paris*,
from blue glass, tasseled with silk.
He had played with the tassel
while she ate the flesh of a fish on a blue plate;
he watched her, remembering her large panties.

She was always in her garden, among the early summer ferns
and purple petunias,
the sprinkler singing water out.

In the morning, under an eiderdown comforter,
his feet in the warm place, he could hear a heavy black engine
passing through the railroad yards heading to Chicago.
in the whine of the shrill whistle.

She made lemonade and potato salad,
a picnic on the SS *Ramona* on Reeds lake,
the sound of brass pistons hissing,
and Milly, his mother's cousin, his playmate
(he had seen her, at his grandmother's funeral, married,
a white, more pale woman, kind), never speaking.

Now he calculates the length of time passed since her dying,
mixing the number of years
with the vision of dinner, the flesh of the white fish,
in an empty restaurant
only two days before.
Half a century strikes a fear.
The house has settled
the foundation down more into the earth.

But it stood; he had seen it once three years ago,
not sure if it was the house or the one next door;
but said to himself, "Yes, I saw it,"
and rid himself the queen of spades.

II. The Photograph the Afternoon of Halloween on Rena Street

In the garden in back of the house he, then the child, for the first time, wore a dress
and felt the elegance against his thighs;
his friends silent; a photograph of his smile
and contentment exists someplace in this house
within a musty cardboard box,
showing always the pleasure of silk against his pure thighs,
like a breath blowing up.

He wonders what the other children in the picture dream tonight,
if ever dream at all and turn down such a street:
perhaps it was only for him—
this solitary journey and the recollection
of the song he sang in his Halloween dress.

Now to bed, to read the last pages of *The Night Train to Lisbon*,
with the sound of rain falling on Rena Street,
dripping down the summer leaves of lilac.
He is uncertain which book to read next
or dream through enigma and layers of time,
murmured of what will never be again: the inevitable oblivion,
the silence of a pin dropping from a violet dress.

2006

II

NATURE AND INCARNATION

The Red Geranium, Seen from My Study Desk

Among the concrete statues: the boy with the apple, boy with the book,
and boy with a cluster of grapes;
the summer red geranium, once atop the wicker table on the patio,
bloomed into early winter on a maple tree branch,
high enough to escape the killing low frosts.
The roots clumped in black soil, clutched and held,
surviving with sufficient season's rain.

When I threw it out, up high in early autumn to tumble down the ravine,
the soil packed firm, root bound, in flight free of the clay pot,
the plant was snatched, caught by branches, hidden behind the crimson leaves,
all unknown to me.

Now with naked trees, the camouflage dropped leaf by clustered leaves,
the plant with green leaves and three red blossoms, hanging upside down,
as if a part of the lightly swaying branch, speaks,

"No, I will not go,"
and so remained 'til All Saints' Day.

Then later, I was startled
to see it gone away.

A coming winter wind had won.

2009

Christmas Eve Morning and the Moon

In darkness, at 5:30 AM, I took Robert, my three-season lover, to the plane.
The first tracks in snow. I followed them, still single tracks, back home.

Staring into the questions of a blue sky;
no answer today, only a shallow vacuity,
and deeper that love should end
in the fast ascent of a Northwest Orient flight.
That plane has undone me with a new moon.

I emptied his still warm coffee cup,
forbidding to raise it to my lips,
and fell into the silence, the dark morning of Christmas Eve.
"Where is my childhood?" I spoke to the reflection in the glass.
No answer.

Large snow falls, gentle beyond this door,
straight down to earth,
marking the return of a heavy season,
carefully blankets the narrow flower beds,
like the graves of children on the Anatolian plains.

The wisteria vines bend over the gray wood wall,
motionless, suspended from another time.
I am fearful, like a traveler to some distant place,
the edge of the road unknown.

* * *

That night, in other darkness,
driving back from Holland, Michigan,
fast on the expressway,
the Nativity and Solstice celebrated,
at rest,
I could not take my eyes
from the beauty of the same moon,
the permanence in all seasons stable,
a firmly fixed light.

I would never die
for fear of losing the whiteness
of the winter moon.

1980

A Breath

This breathing in and out, gasping, blowing,
and whispering soft to caress downy hair—
some divinity unknown to us, untouched, unheard, a mystery:
A god of many names,
this Hebrew Jehovah breathed into Adam,
and the man breathed out.

I know breathing's power of those I love on my neck or face to kiss;
or breathing stirred to heavy passion's bliss,
or soft breathing out of a kitten on my cheek,
and even breathing a deceit to death.

* * *

That summer, the cherry floors were being put into the new house.
Red geraniums hung in baskets on the porch.
While I was in Prague, the sparrow darted back and forth,
between the hanging basket and the lawn;
gathering grass and twigs she built a home
beneath a branch of red geraniums,
safe place concealed and gently rocking in a wind.

But the carpenters put their saw to scream
and cut through their planks on the porch;
When I returned,
I looked into the basket
and saw the nest; the mother flown away.

There were two faltering sparrows, naked smooth, grotesque.
"They are dead," I thought.
I blew my breath lightly;
they rose unsteady,
stretching out their lavender necks, long, spinally,
their yellow beaks, straight up
for food;
a second time, the same;
but I could no more disturb them
in their dying.

* * *

In the morning, one had fallen to the ground.
I wondered how it had pushed through green leaves to the edge,
only sufficient energy left.

I carried the nest to my garden;
the shaped twigs now lost to fluttering wings,
never lifted to the wind
and buried their naked smallness.

A large sadness came to me:
the tragic mystery of earth,
a deity's gift withdrawn,
an old man's breath mistaken
for soft feathers of a mother's wing.

2005

For Becky Bosckey: The Iris Bed

In March, the green blade cuts up through winter
a knife that separates the earth, making
a furrow for the stalks with buds to open lavender,
gold crowns, and purple petals
marked with primal signatures that name them
the victory over killing winters,
to return again with fragile lips
to which I bend to catch subtle fragrance
and again the wonder of being a flower,
among all creations generated things.

I am the man to worship flowers, the yellow beard,
corolla turned up and down,
with the promise next year, the bud,
all will return.

What is seated deep within the roots,
the urgent coding to be what it is, not willed,
but given by force outside
to make its beauty,
an ancient ordination,
a deathless splendor—
some endless mystery,
teasing?

2013

A Spring Migration and Death

Death on my small porch did not come easy to this wax wing bird:
not Bohemian, but Cedar.
My neighbor and I looked at the green trembling,
fallen at the foot of the moon flower vine:
the tail spread to reveal the yellow band,
a bright arc of light; he too a heavenly planet,
once circling above the horizon, now put low.

I had heard the sound, like a clump of sod against the glass,
deceiving him in flight to this small space
of Anatolian rugs, Chinese incense, a porcelain vase:
Mongolian artifacts, remembered distance and lovers, of which I sing,
but this bird too had come on his journey from Guadalupe,
celebrated on winter berries fermented in the sun,
the journey half flown to Manitoban swamps and cooler air.

Now the wings spread in no-flight; the head lifted to fall again.
Nature's inborn cycle comes to all.
A drop of water, in the beak, glistened in the afternoon light.
I crouched to watch the pointed sharpness open and close,
to hear some silent singing of his wine,
words of another world from which he traveled far,
saw visions other than my own.

While I was in the kitchen, he died; when I looked, he was gone.
The neighbor scooped him up; I know his ways to be rid of things.

Once, these summer days in Michigan to fly above some water,
the constant daring, soft yellow feathers and green
to lure some fish hidden in a cold stream,
with whistling songs of Guadeloupian moons,
and the North Country's bending reeds,
undone by a thick plate of glass,
enticed by dark Mongolian lands.
If it had been for me to put the bird away,
he would rest beneath the climbing vine,
so fly In bud and blossom, lengthen his short day.

1992

From My Study Window: Lorca and the Vanishing Duck Pond

From my window: two ducks in the small pond will vanish before spring departs.
A fallen tree, leafless, fell first from its crown and lay near the silent water.
A short distance from the pond a solitary deer forages for acorns
among the leathered leaves.

The cat is on my desk murmuring pleasures, not looking out the window,
and I, leaning to the light, am at my desk with ducks, a fallen tree, a deer, a sleeping cat,
and book.

I am reading *Federico Garcia Lorca: A Life,*
but I am reading of his death,
the breeze in the land,
his brown eyes, his blood,
and hand that made poetry, smooth images to speak of tragedy.

I glance out, away from the flowering blood,
his eyes turning to marble,
the hand that made poetry trembles and death comes over the line — *duende,*
and a precarious life, a voice comes to an end.

The small pond will vanish when the spring leaves.
The ducks seem not to remember this;
and each early season return to build a nest,
then to abandon when the pond dries up, before any hatchlings are seen.
And the eggs?
I have never looked for fear to find too dark a thing.

This voiceless woods in shadows—
becomes an ancient Grecian stage,
and Lorca too laying in the wings,
just beyond the olive trees,
while the ducks swim around and around on the pond,
knowing nothing of tomorrow, like Lorca,
the day before the rushing train to Andalusia,
the shrill of the whistle, like ancient Sybil's voice.

2005

The Summer Sounds of Winter Water

Grayness stretches down to dead grass
shown through mounds of soot-covered snow.

Late I lifted the wooden blinds
to peer out at night;
past the lamppost light, to splintering flashes
reflected in a shining pool.

"It is cold," I said
and read my book on the Cappadocian plains.

The inner vision of the lyric eye
moved from dead February
to powder resting on the vineyards.
The greenness saved by the sluices of mountain water,
sounding out to dry earth, like falling winter rain.

The soul turned around, away from stinging sleet against the glass,
to ride my horse Sabah into mountain wind and rush of melted streams,
even to Derevenk's Armenian ghosts, Roman bridge and richest grass,
to lay in the sun, put down and rest in other dreams;
or ride the valley out its length to carved caves
and find a chapel lost and murmur in ancient words now gone—
murmur them to sleep.

1995

Madonna Lilies for the Feast of the Epiphany

This buying garden gloves each year:
the color just right the size, yes—these gloves, brown, cheap to throw away;
then to see them again when I am looking for the saw—
and others too at the bottom of the cardboard box, dry dirt—
worn once or never worn, the price tag in place, sometimes white or green,
almost always never worn.

No one in my family wore garden gloves.
My father came into the house with thorn-cuts on his fingers,
a remnant of caked dirt on his palms, sacred evidence:
we knew his melon garden was free of weeds—
the wild blackberries pulled back to a border.
My grandmother Mabel didn't wear gloves either.
She pushed lightly, with soft hands, fragile roots into the soil,
to make lavender cosmos grow.

No, I have never worn garden gloves for more than two minutes.
Earth is what I want to feel: to break the clods, to touch the cold depth,
to scoop soil up when I am planting red geraniums,
or better, planting bulbs,
alone beneath a forever November gray day,
winter bidding and chilling fingers.

* * *

Reverent wonder engulfs all time.
I hold the naked bulb, smooth, perfect,
with the shoot, the bud, the flower of white petals, the fragrance contained
in this silent roundness,
sleeping down all winter.

Thus, I am seduced to lovely mysteries.

No one sees us:
I am alone with the bulb,
and I kiss it,
to kiss all Creation,
Christ Incarnate in my garden earth,
and Mary so inclined to birth.
I kiss again what will be: the bud, white petals, sweet honey,
while breath of Deity
blows winter wind on me
and other promises.

2007

Alpha In the Shadow of the Rock

I.

The Tabernacle
at St Mark's reflects
soft illuminations of the candle still burning within the glass—
two o'clock in the morning:
the white sanctuary lamp:
in shadows
of dark night,
now in cold advent,
promises ancient energies waiting,
in this leafless time of wastelands.

I have not knelt in that place this night,
but dreamed the light.

Closing T. S. Eliot,
putting Mr. Prufrock away,
turning to other wastelands
in which Mr. Ramsay cries out,
"We perish, each alone!"

Or the old man
looking at the purple patterns on his hand,
makes flat the white sheet,
a dry land on his chest;
and he remembers the sound, through the slumbering summers,
of his grandmother's voice calling up from the kitchen
and the distant sound of a steam engine
shrill whistling on the track to Chicago.

Or in this room a fading photograph of Talas
summons reveries to that place in youth and belief
where I made love in the scent of acacia trees:
a stone school built by Turks,
missionaries watching:
a skeleton tree, the summer house,
the veranda with green Adirondack chairs,

the stone walk to the children's cemetery, two graves:
Lois and Robert sleeping these years since 1895
among the iris and lilac returning every spring—
and the bright orange, paper poppy still growing near the edge of the world.

From that place each night
the sun sinks down lower than the cliff-high graves;
and now looking out,
all returns,
            singing the sound
            of the single note on the wet lip of a glass,
            caressed by a finger,
            all turns around more vivid,
            retrieved from oblivion.

II.

I dare not breathe against this Spirit, brushing against me.

III.

In this writing room exists the statue of the boy with a wounded bird:
a feather,
crystal,
shell,
surrounded by candles—icons through which I walk into childhood:
always *puer* wandering along the buckled side walk, never stepping on cracks,
turning autumn leaves over, looking for a fallen bird or something new, a silver
thimble.

IV.

I would hide me down,
breathing litanies,
singing words
in the night,
dreaming of that other place—

the distant gardens of Talas
and the dead children, sleeping, in graves no longer marked,
or cradle lovers in my arms.
with whom once I walked where iris bloomed.

So all is in—gathered beneath that light;
in cold advent all the world is waiting
for something new to happen,
some holy child who will turn the world around,
the splendid cosmic Alpha,
born two thousand times
in each of us, a mystery to be touched
and opened, becoming more than now.

1988

One Easter Lily Blossoms on November 3, 2015, in This Cold Place

Today the garden is dismantled and far flung;
but I have brought into the house a palm, green and grape ivy, a viburnum.
All of the rest:
geraniums, impatience, begonias, and ferns
are tumbled down the ravine.

That tossing is a hard time:
then the pot flies out over the brown oak leaves, spinning down to the pond.
I hear no screams of fear or protest, but I know I toss them to the end—
their few seconds in eternity to live;
once my companions on still mornings,
reading the New York Times—reports on the shedding of fresh blood,
the tearing of flesh; The Solace of Fierce Landscapes: mystic visions,
so of another place and time,
catching images from the ancients in the earth of my small woods,
whispered words of desert saints near the old roots.
In the shadows of the trees, the hopping of a warted toad.

From my study window I watch seasons unfurl, stay a time, and vanish.
Spring forsythia matures to strong yellow,
and white mounds of cascading spirea,
then petals brown in fading,
scatter far on walks near Fountain Cemetery,
to be hustled along the concrete.

Shafts of fern unfurl, the bud shells drop.
leaves spread shades of green,
the sun plays new shadows on the fallen trunks of trees.

The statues stand firm on the veranda:
boy with an apple, boy and a book,
boy with a branch of grapes,
boy listening to the sea in a shell
in autumn blood red and orange—
all are dimensions of being,
hidden during winter days;
the memories of lonely childhood

after supper as dusk turned to dark,
I walked with a stick: tap, tap, turning over leaves
for treasure, a blue jay's feather.

Later, the pots of geranium, begonia, viburnum,
ivy, restored on the stone walls of the fountain—the laughing boy
pours water from his pomegranate
to a warmer sun and whitest clouds.

* * *

Two pots of white lily bulbs from last spring,
neglected during the summer:
outside, not watered,
one tipped over.
Now two green shoots,
late this spring above last year's withered stem, emerged from within the bulb;
to twist and snake up and today November 17, one white lily opens.
Cold nights have prolonged the presence
of petal, stamen, pistol, and pollen.

In dusk, I see white of the once abandoned bulb coming through the ferns.
Having leaned against the elements, the white lily remains perfection,
a flawless fragrance, an image in dark dusk.
In cold November, it is being a lily,
in light snow falling,
a freezing scent.

2015

III

MOMENTS OF BEING

Waiting for the End in My Father's Bleached Hospital Room

In the bleached room, time and dark stains evaporated
like clocks stopped in my childhood,
the very air swallowed up;
now moments passed, unmeasured leisure.

In his immaculate bed,
my father mended socks, sorted screws, planned to paint the ceiling.
He played with the hem of the sheet—his shroud,
turning the white fabric over and over again as if to make it gone,
then let it spring free,
to fold again.

I said, "What are you doing?"
He whispered he was getting the cuff right for ironing.
He had always pressed our Sunday pants to put in a good crease;
and his mother had taught him the trick of pressing the worn seat of pants
with vinegar to take the shine out; it worked,
but on summer church mornings, our sweat made all smell like a brine vat.

He paid no attention to our objections.
His childhood was woven into our lives,
the haircuts in the basement,
or the cuff alongside the head,
scrapping endlessly the last jelly in the jar,
his knife clinking on the glass to drive us mad;
my brother and I were shaped, even as my father.

By his side that last day, there was no putting down of my father's dying work,
but a reverence for what rose up out of poverty:
pants worn by the first boy, the second, the last.

So on his death bed, he ironed, sometimes sorted screws.
He turned them over and over, then tossed them into invisible drawers,
each to the right drawer.
I said, "Are they real?" Not certain, he looked up.
"The ceiling needs painting," he said.

So the day before my father's death there was no easy peace.
I waited for the taut string to break.

At 811 Major Place SE, all four sons born in that house,
cures and a way of living sat in every corner,
lay in every drawer,
existed in every wooden box in the cellar,
history strewn about,
this ancient legacy of fathers, fathers,
and fathers I had not known except in the forming of myself.

When my mother and I arrived, summoned by the nurse at four thirty in the morning,
"If you want to see him alive, you had better come," she had said.
We did.

He had waited with only three more breaths
and lay on his side so we could not see what the fungus had done to his eye
before it crept into his brain.
My mother said, how young he looks.
Did such appearance for her return her lover
and the white sand days at the beach,
the dance Hall by Little Bass Lake?
She really never knew him dead until we had buried him;
and she went home, down to the cellar,
and he wasn't tinkering there with screws and a rusting hinge.
She telephoned me late that night but couldn't speak,
only deep sobbing breaths came to my ear.

I have put the nails and screws on the shelf, a place for sacred things, like seashells
from Ibiza, a stone from the garden wall in Talas, a green ribbon from my love,
a lead bus token to take me from Caesarea of Cappadocia to Wingate Hall,
all beneath my crucifix from Palma.

Oh, my father, my father.

I kissed him on his forehead
for the last time,
the first time.

Sitting with Old Dorothy Stephens on the East Porch at Murray Lake on June 20, 1967

The day was a summer morning forty-eight years ago:
cool June arrived in cobalt water, spring leaves in greens.

The cottage was white, built on the top of a long rise of grass, up from the lake.
We sat on the screened porch.
Weekdays there were no boats, no Mercury motors whining, no Jet-Skiers.
Still water spoke smooth, smelling of iron, strong, eternal in history,
made eons ago: some slide of ice, cutting deep with boulders and stones,
making the crescent shape of the lake, beneath this same sky.
On this day shadowed under great white pines, we sat like soothsayers, easily speaking the truth of the past, claiming in the end the splendor of our lives and a disbelief that we had endured all error and tragedy given to us, but all had shaped and, at times, left us only with an increasing sense vacuity.

The wind in tall north pines is a voice, blowing among tufts of needles and bending twigs, while the low branches tapped the screens and roof. But a sudden gust of violent wind would force us silent, as if perhaps some danger or small event that had been overlooked in our story was returning to our memory and that damage: a word or a slight turning to the right, unbeknown had altered the direction of our lives, or was perhaps approaching now.

We gazed; images blurred before us, a single white sail beyond the willow trees. Only silence existed, the sacred moments of no thoughts, only awareness of a misty inner vision, over laid on the images before us: the irrevocable past, the remembered face, a hand lifted to shade the young man's eyes, all floated in silent currents, just beneath the surface of nothingness and far off places. But the moment existed, without our volition, and the reel of the film stopped for several seconds; it had been only life passing; and the boat with the fluttering white sail turned the point and disappeared.

Shortly after breakfast, the dishes done, the cottage was ours in echoing emptiness, stretching out beyond the reeds to far boarders of the lake.

"Would you like a drink?" she said.
I hesitated. "Nine o'clock? Sure, what the hell."
"Just two fingers of whiskey and one ice cube."
So the chalice was prepared, lifted, and the chanting of the liturgy begun.

We owned the opulence of our lives, the irony, the romance, and sorrow;
we knew youth had long past; the same fate as day lilies, irreversible.

Suddenly, she spoke of childhood, her grandmother planting flowers on family graves,
carefully sorting Joseph's coat, Jacob's ladder, with white petunias, red geraniums, lavender sweet alyssum, each plant according to the likes of the woman dead, so many years, beneath the rural sod. "Then we had to go to another cemetery." She laughed. She continued. "We don't plant flowers for the dead but for ourselves. The moments of planting filled and blending to some unutterable affection that sustained a reverence for our lives, an unrelenting fog of incomprehension, but eventual bonding and surrender."

The words fell out with the clinking sound of ice in the glasses, still early in the morning.
The rising smoke from Kent cigarettes, was drawn quickly up by the wind,
rushed out the rusting screens.

She said, "My father built this place, everything: the plumbing, the wiring; and he planted all the trees, built the dock. He did all of this." She lifted her head and looked above the lake, as if something were still there. "Years later, he had cancer, after my mother had died." She stopped; the pause gave time to focus on the fact. "He killed himself; he had called Metcalf Mortuary, and said that someone had died. His car was in the drive, right up there. He had attached the hose to the pipe and then put it through the window. Later in the afternoon, Mike moved the car and found a half-eaten almond cake on the dashboard."

All was simple fact. No more details were requested, no questions were to be asked. The story was complete.

After some silence, she said, "I don't think it was wrong, do you?"
I said, "Oh no . . ." And we sat looking at the ducks among the reeds and a soaring hawk, light on the wind, above all the world. It was a bird, and death was death. Hazy blue smoke drifted out of the screens. And ice cubes clinked, like brass bells, and we tapped ashes into the crystal ashtray, left out all winter, with the snow blowing in through the screens, like a white dust, not melting 'til March. We didn't speak for a long time.

* * *

In the great luxury of the those quiet days at the lake, all seemed brought to a clarity. The vision held between grief and joy. What once was, remained for us to wonder at.

"Dorothy, did I ever tell you about Koray, my Byzantine prince?"
"No." She laughed, low and brief. These stories of lovers or would-be lover always seemed to her enigmatic illusions. Or perhaps the laugh was just a moment of comic relief, like the fourth act of a Shakespearean tragedy.

"The last time I saw him was at the college, a senior. I had final appointments in my office with all of my senior students. We talked about his plans at the university. There would be no drama, no theater, no arts. He would leave who he was at his parents' wish. He left. I could hear him walking down hall and called out, 'Koray.'"
"Sir?" he said.
"I will remember you."
"Yes sir."
He continued walking.
I hear the sound of his heels on the marble floor, the exact sound, even now.

I had meant to say, "Come, come to the Yilgin River. The current will take us out to sea."

I stared at the lake, blue moving,
while speaking again of the gardens of Talas in Turkey, the death of Koray—
long after we had sat on the white sand at the abandoned beach in Mersin.
I spoke of his artwork, the play he had written, and mentioned my
returning to America. He stood and started to run down the hard sand.
"Come, come to the river where Cleopatra's barge entered.
We will ride the current into the sea."
With terrifying urgency, we dove in, and the Yilgin River took us out to the sea.

"I wonder if after I was home that first year, knowing more the strength and depth of my love, all would have been different.
He was shot just a few years later in Ankara."

"Ah yes,"
we would say,
"perhaps so,
or maybe there would have been no difference,"
a fallen voice.

We knew that these single happenings determined all the rarities of our lives
and bent our days in peculiar portents.

The words spoken set the souls at a balanced peace of disbelief. It was an easy
moving of time on the blue lake, while whiskey stung the tongue,
blue smoke vanished into the day,
and the white bow of the ship, SS *AKdeniz,*
swung into the vast currents of the Mediterranean Sea—
a voyage to a distant land, perhaps Byzantium.

1970–2015

The Enigmatic Loveliness of Three Butterflies in Summer

I.

Today, in search of milkweed's lavender,
a monarch polonaised by this window sill,
so close, but for the screen, it would have entered in.
Vision held erratic movements of orange,
outlined in dust -white and black, a
a Rouault painting, with lead relief,
this art of stained glass flying from St. Vitus,
a butterfly with brief winging time divine.

II.

Yesterday I saw one monarch wing,
fragile art broken on hot asphalt in the parking lot.
How had it come to be at this mall?
No sweet lavender grows here for miles around.
Then I saw the last of the journey traveled free,
on a grill . . . mouth like to swallow,
where clung the rest divine;
flight interrupted from milkweed to milkweed,
after crossing country roads in search of silken honey,
to die unquenched, making small disaster large.

III.

This morning, Jakub, dark lover—after long journey away from your passion,
like stained glass: yellow, violet, cobalt, blood-red, all moving colors,
in the windows of St. Vitus and the paradise bar,
I remember your winged arms of olive flesh,
dancing your lean beauty in flight,
caught within a dark room of hazy smoke where each night
I waited for you, your reaching to strangers, pulling in
red light and lavender scent to your sweating body,

holding in fragile love, invented creature dreamed divine,
now wings away, translucent beyond the sea
in this God's autumn order of vanishing splendor.

2002

A Keeping Place for Photographs and Old Notes

I am setting right,
straightening drawers, putting order to shelves;
I find the tokens, the icons of my past placed between books, and pages in books;
back in cluttered drawers, old shoe boxes: photographs, words on notepaper, a
lapel pin of my father's: a service pin in gold and blue, speaking his years
of hard work for the Chesapeake and Ohio Railroad;
we couldn't talk religion, without tedious argument,
so talking ceased.

I discovered this morning a photograph taken in Greece, on white sand,
bordering the dark blue water; the horizon lifted a glass bowl of lighter blue.
I am sitting next to a handsome Greek, with black hair wet from the sea;
he has a wild knowing look, laughing, squinting in the sun.
I am wearing a black bathing suit, he nothing;
in my right hand, I have a Kent cigarette—
and now I remember the sweetness of the tobacco, after a year of cheap cigarettes.
Between the Greek and me lifted up the ambiance of a gentle innocent lust;
we knew we had caught each other for the night—it was easy and sinless,
removed three thousand miles from the harsh sermons of my early youth.

Tucked between the pages of a book, I see again a note given to me in New York,
just before the white liner SS *Independence* sailed for Casablanca, Palma Majorca,
Naples, and then on the *San Marco* to Piraeus, and places beyond, until Byzantium,
the Church of Holy Wisdom and the Mosque of Sultan Ahmet turned to gold.

My mother had written, "I know that this is the day for which you have dreamed . . .
write to us. We will need to hear from you."

I wrote, but for me, the city from which I came no longer existed. The vast land of
Turkey, the sound of the call to prayer from a minaret in a small Anatolian village,
the spice bazaars, the handsome Turks on the ferry on the Bosporus, wooed me
away from solemn days and places to myriads of new beauty and *soul-clapping
hands*.

Last winter, I found a poem from a student in a British literature class, Stephen, who
said he sometimes at night could hear my voice reading poetry—"the sound like
the flight of a butterfly," he said. He was beautiful.

A copy of James Barrie's novel *A Window in Thrums*, given to me by my grandfather. The book has a green cover, imprinted with golden bamboo poles and wound among them, a vine of blanched green leaves and pale flowers. Jamie arrives back to the weavers' cottage too late for his mother Jesse to see him again, after years of waiting—a sentimental story and agrarian warning of the dangers of the city.

Inside the book is the notice of my grandfather's death in January 1957.

Later, after his burial,
I drove back to the cemetery;
the red carnations on the fresh grave
were frozen sharp as a blade to my touch,
melting before they could cut—
the cleanest January afternoon: sun, clear sky, ice, a black crow cawing,
an ordinary day.

These are holy things held with the wafer of Christ's body, kissed; gifts from God,
lifted in silence, then returned to a wooden tabernacle,
beneath a burning candle in red glass—a keeping place;
in my mind, it is so.

August 2008

Tone: Lines on Hands

I.

My father's hands were lovely, slender fingers
and longer nails than usual for a man who worked outdoors:
maintaining switches and signals for the Pere Marquette Railroad,
then the Chesapeake and Ohio.

After his death, my mother and I
were going through drawers in his chest—
an invasion of my father, I thought.
I discovered in the corner of a drawer, a small jar
half filled with nail clippings.
"Why would he do such a thing?" I said.
My mother said, "He kept his nail clippings,"
as if it were an embarrassing oddity—to be kept secret, so to fear.
I said, "It was his orderliness; his neatness."
But I don't know.
He held his plow, lifted tomatoes,
and had graceful penmanship—
all consistent in beauty.

II.

My grandmother's hands were lovely:
soft, silken, with dark blue veins raised—
a diamond on one finger.
Her nails shinned—little marble swirls.
As a small boy, I would lift her hand in church,
looking, looking,
and pinching her skin into little flesh tents,
then watch them flatten out;
"Look, little tents," I said.
She quickly put her hand
into her white laced glove.

Now I have tents.

III.

My mother's hands were soft
and when she was dying, and I sat beside her bed,
I held her hand with my two hands, the palm and the face.
The dying had been for hours.

And I rested my head on the bar that kept her in the bed.
The room was silent but for her lightest breathing
and the small whisper of the oxygen.
So close to her arm, I smelled the fragrance of her body:
the scent I knew as a child.

IV.

Our priest has hands of strength, with a gold canon's ring,
lifted above the chalice and the paten: the wine and bread,
he blesses with his hands and says the words, a mystery: "Body and Blood."
And Christ comes down incarnate,
his hands healing.
All of this happens beneath a stained window of a crowned Shepherd King:,
cobalt and red, showing his pierced hand and orb.
"So be it," I say.

V.

1962: Maria, a short woman, aging, in a black dress with a clean white apron, cooked all the meals on a coal stove without a breeze in the small kitchen at the pension in Ibiza, Spain. She was a very quiet woman, who spoke only once to me. I was twenty-one, confident and cocky.

While drinking too much wine with my friends at lunch, I said, "Show me the palms of your hands. I tell fortunes." Each prediction was a high joke; we laughed and chocked.

Maria came to the table. "Tell me my fortune."

Her palm was worn with deep cresses and rough. No cream had ever touched them.

"More work, then an easier time." She was content, smiled.

I felt such a grieved ass.

In the late afternoon, with our towels, we went to the rocks to swim
in luxury and kinky fortunes,
an uneven providence.

VI.

My hands on the knuckles are rough and slightly red.
They, like my imagination, have been many places,
even needle pointing with Jeremy,
so clean a sweep of thread.
I spread the fingers apart and look down at each and the palm.
Startled, I can't imagine them dead.

"Not to think of," my housekeeper would say to me.

2015

IV

EPIPHANIES

The Villa in the Algarve

Sometimes birds fly away
when Hattie comes through the French doors opening to a valley of parched grass,
the scent heavy in moistures of morning,
the fragrance gone before noon.

Hattie, Hattie, what are you doing?

She barks them away, I say;
the small birds pecking at the veranda tiles.

Marjorie wants me to play the *Death of the Dauphin,*
Ravel's grieving line of notes out to the sea.

But it is only morning, I say.

The record player would utter our separate names,
places, even destinies fragmented—
we are people of partings: how many times the overnight train, the plane,
waving a handkerchief, tapping the umbrella on the window pane, a lifted hand;
tomorrow it will be the Marmara Sea,
or the twisted red leaves of October blowing through the park in Ankara,
tumbling, tumbling away; we laugh.

Now we sit with gin, tonic, green lime, the clink of ice
in the crooked shade of this new place: the white villa
with the round yellow sun
in the Algarve.

Half a glass and I put it away;
we stare out to another place.
What does she see, I wonder:
the vision changing from pines in the valley
to the high mountains of Caesarea,
the snow slow melting all the summer,
the rivulets, spilling through the garden sluices:
cobalt marbles, rolling, rolling away?

Marjorie wants me to play the *Death of the Dauphin*.
It would be right for our coming and going to different lands,
these long separations.

But it is only morning, I say.

We talk about horses—
yes, yes, I say, Cesur and Sabah
riding in the mountains where Armenians once hid in the caves.
We talk about the sound of hooves on hard dirt roads,
the rhythm of the iron shoes—
each hearing what we heard,
paradise in the valley of Derevenk,
where the Romans built a bridge,
near green poplars in the wind.

Our arrivings and leavings,
without warning,
after thirty-seven years.

Or more, she says.
Her light dressing gown, gold silk,
spider woven, lifted by the wind.

In those days, Pan American could fly me to the past,
where Marjorie sat in her orange grove.
We seldom went any place,
sitting at the breakfast table,
or among the trees and hanging fruit—the citrus scent of it;
or on the veranda,
the coolness of the morning coming up to our feet.

So we are reciting again the litany of the falling sun,
cold shadows against the high cliffs,
the horses tearing the spring grass;
the light dappled in the olive grove,
and the sound of a hammer striking stone,
like the ringing of a heavy Sanctus bell,
a requiem echoing out within the deep valley,
from thirty years ago
for weary walking Armenians.

Marjorie wants me to put the *Death of the Dauphin* on the record player,
right for our coming and going, the years in between.
But sometimes we went dancing under the carnival light, outdoors,
in the cool of the summer night.

You made marmalade for me to take home—
oranges from your orchard.
Do you remember?

We would say yes
or no we went down to the village.
Yes, yes, it was the town, the other would nod.
So we looked out for time to come,
or time to go;
or stay, she dared say.

So drinking gin in the Algarve,
we chanted the litany of our being on the Anatolian plains,
in the wounded wing sound in autumn—
in the flight of a thousand white cranes.

2000

Morning Consciousness in June

Printed doves fly in lines across the bed sheets:
pastels of gray, beige, and cream,
one flock East, the other West,
and we in between,
an echo comes from Tarsus pines
away—1965,
locked in romantic cells of youth:
the touch of warm flesh drawn.

Never changing direction, no turn-around in dreams,
relentless in the wing-working, the air pushed down,
the doves up, in ethereal streams.

It is all this: an imagining, fair luck to see the folly of a prayer,
but consent and know ever in earth, Madonna Lilies, the soft belly of a cat
a star whose light is still to come,
hope to another, food, a book, one's body to another, or sweet music in E flat major;
Who hears prayer?
Who knows incarnation without our touch?

An icon is enough to enter through a moving sun.

Half awake, half asleep, to take some indolence in a June morning,
window open, and a caressing breeze on flesh,
this peculiarity freely given:
of doves flying East, doves flying West,
keeping ancient secrets,
and I in emptiness, full being,
with shuttered shadows on the wall.

2015

Wind in High Trees: Changing Voices

I.

This naked man who lost his youth,
now in late night walked the house in sounds of full tongued wind—
Hebrew voices weeping psalms of Babylon among the bark and leaves of autumn
trees.
He couldn't see but listened;
if seeing would have been,
he had gazed
the last of summer torn from the gripping twigs.

Morning confirmed:
yesterday held branches full
of orange and burgundy.
November razed the trees;
and limbs, like the veins of a corpse laid against the sky;
all blown out of season

II.

The yellow beauty:
mellow autumn fled;
and in its place the tilting voice of somber dead
in wind borne high
until the sky bled out all discord.

His ancient ancestors forever knew: the onslaught of cold and ice;
the voice of geese, wing-lapping on the air;
and on the barren bushes nothing sweet to tongue or soul remained,
as if incarnation drew back to some other design.

III.

He, a boy, out in November dusk, had wandered empty streets,
his stick turning leaves,
looking always for feathers and stones,
to line a cultic shrine on the sill with three white bones.
to fly in the wind to high trees,
like some ancient priest murmuring recurring riddles.

IV.

Now the old man, who walked the house in last night's dimness,
with invalid's vision glances left and right at a silent past,
with small statues and busts of men
who seldom spoke, Russian boxes of cranes ascending,
a cup with three keys to where, and in the corner the photograph of Koray, the dark boy
raven hair and eyes—long dead,
haunting all his life.
Thy swam in Cleopatra's river, the current
taking them out to sea;
and the old man remembered later the white sand blown against the boy's wet thigh,
burning sun, drying the black hair to tremble.

V.

He stood naked in the dark and wondered
what purpose should lead him to the end,
what liturgy of hope sung by a voice
among high trees or stars
in these last days of bent history;

VI.

What wonder to fall upon:
the distance between darkness,
suns,
ever opening more infinity;
while Mary, crowned with stars
in her blue kimono,
above the crescent moon, rising,
sings words of mythic mysteries—
in the hour of our death,
her womb again conceiving.

2009

Chen from Shanghai

Twisting oak leaves scatter in autumn's wind, pursuing and fleeing each other

> In the china cabinet on the east wall of the dining room
> is a small porcelain statue of the great Chinese poet Li Bai of the Tang
> Dynasty.
> With him two boys play instruments:
> one stroking two strings, the other whistles his long flute
> while Li Bai drinks wine and writes poetry,
> holding a china cup.
> Inside the figurine is a curled, brittle letter from David;
> he was leaving twenty-nine years ago.

Now Chen from Shanghai,
as surging sea waves, cresting a flash dash down beneath the moon,
chants a poem by Li Bai, intoning:

> "Moon light shoots over the bed
> like snow on the ground
> head up to see the moon
> head down to the ground
> thinking of my village and home,"

while among the crystal glasses
the porcelain children play out notes,
somber songs of a melody, creating itself
like fine silver spoons striking lightly
on antique cups, not shattering.

Twisting oak leaves like two frightened pilgrims on different paths flee,
taking sacred stories of vanished love far beyond the sea.

2011

The Girl in the Pink Coat Skating on Turner Street

I met her on the west side of the city.
A friend warned me, "Be careful walking there";
I saw no danger, only gray houses, upholstered chairs on porches,
grotesque rusted cars in yards, a flat dead cat, window screens broken out, even glass;
all things tilted out of balance.

On this day, she came around the corner on skates, a whiz:
what a child of seven or ten, her body in full swoops, not grace,
a grimmest face, all energy against a world that put her in that place.
Her coat was a burden she neglected to button, pink with dirt smudges,
too big for her, hanging below her knees, almost touching the skates.
What had someone said? "Put your coat on,"
or just at first she felt the cold, put it on, her sister's coat,
now hers for spring.

The metallic click of her skates on slanting pieces of sidewalk stopped;
she tottered in front of me, arms akimbo, no hands showing.
From her red-cheeked face, she said, "What are you doing walking on our street?"
"Just going for a walk."
"Want to see me do a trick?"
"Yes."
"Watch!"
She made a jump, turned a circle, jolted precariously straight, swayed again.
"Well, that's my skating trick," marveling in wonder at her art.
Then widened her eyes, muscled out her legs and said to all the street,
"Someday I am going to be the roller-skating queen of the world."
Enough of me, she whirled away.

This afternoon, years gone, I wonder what happened to her,
that laughing
spring zephyr in pink, fleeing
from Turner Street.

2006

Sitting by My Window, Looking at a Photograph of Talas

I am outside this photograph,
looking in at the stone wall, the vineyard,
the framing acacia trees,
through the hazy distance between myself and Wingate Hall,
as if I am on the stone road, walking to school in the early days of May.
My magnifying glass in my hand moves steady across the inches
of the picture and the miles of space to another place
on the Anatolian plains, near the fields of Kayseri.
I do not breathe for fear that breathing will move my hand too quickly,
and I should fail to see some boy with his book,
sitting on the wall, where names are carved into the soft rock;
or not remember some teacher gazing out to the Yilanli Mountains,
in the long shadows of sunset,
although, having looked before, I know they are not there.

The fading colors, lavender and wheat, shape images just beyond my reach:
the kiosk with vacant windows looking back at me,
and quiet yards, filled once with the sound of young boys,
hold haunts and the elusive silence of time, emptied out to the purple mountains,
beyond to centuries, the vast forever past, unfurling.

Moving the glass, I know beyond the trees exist the gardens
and water sluices running in the late coolness of the afternoon.
Cook prepares the dinner and students make noise in mischief,
or breathe in silently, moving pencils across paper to make some meaning.

The clear air fills with the scent of the small white flowers of the acacia tree,
and all time is one time: comradery, task, the melding of two cultures,
the darting of the barn swallows in summer dusk,
then and now, that vision and this window, dissolving thirty-one years;
and I, in this moment, am in that place. None is lost. All is more.
I walk again in the garden, and ride my white horse Sabah into the endless valley
of Derevenk beyond the Roman bridge and row of green poplars,
where once I heard the sound of a hundred sheep passing.

Do any in Talas, on such nights, know that I am there, any child at games, woman walking home, or man reading the newspaper by the window, look up to know that love descends and time is surrendered away?

1995

A Slide from Ibiza

Always the film in the drawer holds the memory exact, images of the place intact.

In January, every three years, unexpectedly, I come across the slide,
hold it to the winter night, squint in, focus on the sand, sea, and breaking wave,
quite startled to see us young again, caught unmoving, in never ending light.

We were building a sand castle; Tuson bends to lift the wet sand,
Arna searches for a shell; three ships, horizon locked,
gently ride the swell of sea.

Beyond the grass, Madame Argot, who made this island her poetry for eighty
years, sleeps in the sun to rest, while green lizards walk on the wet sand,
covering her ancient breasts.

Somewhere behind the palm trees is a basket of bread, wine and cheese,
in a cool shadow no one sees.
I placed it there.

Quite out of distance, over the low hill, is the blue carriage and white horse
to take us back to town
where love stands for me in the dark night,
beneath the olive trees.

Never in all these years did the head of the horse lift,
the sand fall, the shell be found, or the ships sail free,
nor Madame Argot awaken to scatter the lizards to the grass,
but sleeps on in arrested sun, as if all were done.

I wonder if beneath the olive tree he ever waits for me,
or hears the sea breaking on the pebbles and in murmurings drawback
as I hear in this dark night, or sees the swirling snow, from a distance,
so far in years.

2002

To Darryl: Splintered Ice

January, after summer's love is lost;
a cold like death is in the leafless wood,
where now the season like the sun spins swooned;
and late at night beneath the winter's haloed moon,
hoar frost skeletoned on every branch,
sorrows out to wreathe in terror your name.

You went back to Los Angeles.

I inquired once.
Your aunt said, "Dead,
his father never spoke to him."

I suspicioned so.
Now the word scrawled
on a floating shoal,
wedged quick against the rocks,
the sound of splintering and echoing
never silent, this death, never foreseen
where once we gathered shells
and sea glass polished blue and green.

I saw love vanish in October, soon after summer made your face
netted out with desire—
August's gift among Queen Anne's lace
in heat, not this cutting ice
to stretch to ages coming,
never to be rewoven again in Summer's Spring.

The soft fabric of those days torn, uneven in winter's sway.
Your warm breathing, an artic vapor,
drifts beneath aurora's light, too far away.

2002

Jeremy's Irises, Roses, Plums, and Orange-Pink Peaches on Black Porcelain

This is to inform you
the iris were open this morning when I awoke,
making their delicate blueness and yellow,
a short-lived beauty,
separated in a glass vase—
from the roses away,
which remained held by the black porcelain,
with lavender plums
and light orange-pink peaches.
The roses are unfurling more a brightness,
in this room of dark books,
where murmuring memories return
of islands,
distances,
and faces,
in a cutting out of words
to make meanings—
to say,
"I am this
in the soft beauty
of a gray day
illumined
by iris and roses
in glass
and porcelain."

All of this happens while the iris open,
and we stand in the dancing shadows watching.
Nothing is resolved, while the vision evolves and vanishes,
but the iris and roses are certain.

2001

Perspectives: My Grandfather William's Green Boat and the Purple Dragon Flies in March 12, 2006

This photograph, an icon opens to long pathways,
far into the north woods: roots, branch bark,
vines; and the veins of my grandfather's hand holding a fishing rod,
the line spinning out.

All is suspended in place, whole within a universe of clouds, pine, sun,
the still rich brown the lake, and streams to deeper mysteries, even to death.

My grandfather William's green boat drifts on Peacock Lake;
the silence shattered twice by single drops of water falling from the oar
and wood ground on wood lightly, the paddle raised;
we glided in among the lily pads.

Then, I the child in 1943, sat on the bottom of his boat,
my chin resting on the side, eyes staring out into soft greens.
I had promised I would be silent, sit still.
My grandfather, not once looked at me, but always at the pole
and the water rippling out from the line, not speaking.
The sun, on angle, shimmered the lake,
breaking the shadow shapes of the woods,
the edge a lace of darkness
on water.

I wondered these long-time years why an image of dragon flies
skimming the surface of a pond to my eyes was my remembrance
of the cottage, Whip-Poor-Will, the name above the door:
and only sixty-two years late recollected
I saw them first with my grandfather:
I, the small boy,
peering out above the edge.

Now these years passed
gather in silent calm of winter:
greener, with purple dragon flies
darting, hovering,
just above the surface of a lake.

Then all the world was mine in quiet unfolding:
the summer morning,
doves in soft sorrow grieved the moment passing.
But the child did not know the measure of time,
only that mornings were forever,
while one dragon fly, a flame of burning glass,
in white heat,
rested on his hand,
in wonder to the air,
not shattering.

My grandfather William's green boat
drifts among the lily pads at Peacock Lake.

After great family debate in 1945, I was allowed to see him again
in his black-forest-green casket,
like his row boat,
only velvet and silk:
I was lifted up, to my chin on the edge to peer in at him,
awed again by the beauty of his silent stillness.
The rich scent of lilies,
all humming in the soft sound of dragon flies hovering,
above a green boat,
still drifting, even now,
among the lily pads.

March 12, 2006

A Childhood Memory from the Cottage on Peacock Lake: Age Seven

What is left behind is buried deep within: the calling out of yard geese;
the iron mournful throbbing of the old pump,
aching out from deep within, first the water's iron rust,
the gurgling up, to the gush spilling over the chipped, enameled cup,
even on my belly, gasping;
the sound of bells ringing,
hanging around the necks of old cows sauntering to the barn,
stirring up dust, a low cloud around their hooves,
striking the wooden bridge, the sound hollow, hollow,
the hot day was ending.

All speaks back from the summer of 1943.

Two years later, my grandfather,
after fishing for bass from his green boat,
in the soundless morning of two red winged blackbirds bending on reeds, swinging
lightly, died on his walk back to lunch.
My grandmother found him in the dust,
holding firmly the stringer of fish, sun shining bright,
two red-winged black birds some distance in silent flight.

* * *

I saw him: still, laid out on silk,
clean, groomed in a dark brown suit, a work of art
at Metcalf's on Cherry Street.

The place of the mortuary, now an upper end furniture store
with lovely objects to browse.
Yesterday I stood in the room where I saw him then;
the woodwork, door frames, and leaded windows all the same,
now Windsor Cottage, renamed,
and carefully examined a Chinese vase,
in that same chamber,
but another time: geese calling out,
pump water spilling in dust,
making a rusted lace around my feet;

and suddenly, on the 6th of July, 1945, my grandmother Kate entered in,
so short in a heavy black coat and satin hat,
walked over and kissed his forehead—
my grandfather who was dead.

I was seven again
in an alien place,
and what was left behind, buried deep within, came back,
a gentle haunting:
red wings on a reed
a black satin hat;
and bought the gold gilded porcelain from the East,
fleeing.

2013

V

THE EROTIC INCARNATION

Commentary

From the chapter "The Other Victorians"

For a long time, we supported a Victorian regime, and we continue to be dominated by it even today. Thus, the strange image of the imperial pride is emblazoned, strained, mute, and hypocritical sexuality.

At the beginning of the seventeenth century, a certain frankness was still common, it would seem. Sexual practice had little need of secrecy; words were said without undue reticence, and things were done without too much concealment; one had a tolerant familiarity with the illicit. Codes regulating the coarse, the obscene, and the indecent were quite lax compared to those of the nineteenth century. It was a time of direct gestures, shameless discourse, and open transgressions, when anatomies were shown and intermingled at will, and knowing children hung about amid the laughter of adults: it was a good time when bodies "made a display of themselves."

But twilight soon fell upon this bright day, followed by the monotonous night of the Victorian bourgeoisie. Sexuality was carefully confined; it moved into the home. The conjugal family took custody of it and absorbed it into the serious function of reproduction. On the subject of sex, silence became the rule. The legitimate and procreative couple laid down the law. The couple imposed itself as a model, enforced the norm, safeguarded the truth and reserved the right to speak while retaining the principle secrecy. A single locus of sexuality was acknowledged in social space as at the heart of every household, but it was a utilitarian and fertile: the parents' bedroom. The rest had only to remain vague; proper demeanor avoided contact with other bodies and verbal decency sanitized one's speech. And sterile behavior carried the taint of abnormality; if it insisted on making itself too visible; it would be designated accordingly and would have to pay the penalty.

From: Michel Foucault, *The History of Sexuality*

***

Why has there been such a veritable explosion of discussion about sex in the West since the seventeenth century? How did we ever come to believe it would make us less repressed?

From: Christopher Lasch, *Psychology Index*

* * *

Our sexuality today seems to define what we are; and the *shadow* in the woods, enigmatic sex, continues to speak ambiguously to us, causing political unrest, repression, guilt, erupting in violence, and even death. And the Christian divine, the holy, the Word Incarnated continues to have little do with it; the flesh remains an enigmatic riddle still controlled by ancient definitions of morality. Spirituality is to be understood as above sex.

The ancient Western duality remains: flesh and spirit are separated. Sexual desire and expression are controlled and limited, resulting in the repression of homosexuality. Even the language used in discussing homosexuality or celebrating it is prescribed.

Lawrence Manglitz, 2016

The First Night in Prague

Late that night, we took a streetcar
from the Brevnov Monastery to the first bar—
remote part of the city:
dark, cold, damp, stores closed,
no one other than us on the sidewalks.
I was very excited about the prospects of the evening.
But after a few minutes inside the bar, I said to my friend,
"I don't understand this place. Let's go."

We stood in cold darkness, gloom settling, not speaking.
The night was desolate, soundless, not even a street car.

Later, we found the Escape to Paradise Bar.

But in that moment standing outside waiting,
I had despaired.

Tonight, in this severe city where I have lived long, remembering that evening:
my friend's help,
later meeting Jakub in the dancing red shadows of Paradise—
now sitting here at my study window looking at the fury of winter in gray dusk,
I, am smothered with a same standing, waiting for a street car in an abandoned street.

But then the pleasure in Paradise, within the red flames, returns
dancing with Jakub, the slender gypsy from Bohemia;
I cannot measure the distance back to that time;
it frightens me to see the garden fill with snow.

But that night existed and love was.
I hold the passion above many winter winds,
to heat of red flames dispelling all time,
dancing in the smoothness of his nakedness.

1985

A Gold Icon in the City of Prague: To Jakub the Dancer in the Paradise Night Club

My words, anything I have given you,
are not equal to what you have given me:
> the sweet scent of your body after a night of dancing,
> your flesh a silken gold,
> your lips to taste of sea salt,
> and the sacred moment
> when you kindled within me the heat of lust:
> and love emptied out; I called
> Jakub, Sweet Christ.

I know now in these last years of life,
my short time of consciousness in this eternal cosmos:
> the utter beauty of swirling currents in a river;
> dancing leaf shadows on a crumbled wall of stone,
> the startling, sudden, sound of a bird singing out
> in winter dusk when all the land is ice,
> and the flicker of Christ's candle
> above the polished tabernacle.

What amazement, what holy gifts,
this loveliness coming to me,
and I say more loveliness:
> the perfection of your fingers, moving beneath my kisses;
> your breathing out God's breath on my neck;
> your lashes curved, the dark eyes into which I fell;
> your chest with fine black hair;
> your nipples caressed while you slept,
> softly moving in my arms a dancer still.

I did not sleep, but gazed in wonder all the night,
at flesh and soul named Jakub.

Our lovemaking had been a mystery, a salvation:
        your arching cock, curving out to quench my thirst;
        your flesh given to feed my hunger satisfied.
        Know how sacred—a Eucharist, your gifts to me.
        Know I will on winter nights call out again:
        Jakub, Sweet Christ,
        my Christ.

Such loveliness are those names,
forever beyond the shining shimmer
of white gold around your neck.

Prague, 2006

For the Young Man from Mumbai
Who Worked at Dunkin Donuts

This morning, lifting the cup to my lips, the clean fragrance of coffee,
sweet savor on my tongue, mingled bitterness,
still remaining in the steam that warms my face, I see you move about this room;
you lie beside the edges.

My eyes are out of focus as I stare into the vapors of sun on white bricks
and the sweep of lawn, slightly rising to a hill of pines;
I am seeing into this day of open sky,
while in clusters of three, the leaves drop down among the ivy,
and once again, I plan my beckoning of handsomeness,
your moistened lips of lavender.

In the shop, I have watched your hands pick up the doughnuts
and in detached condescension, drop them into the bag
for those who only speak of doughnuts:
manager's special, old-fashioned.
You are a robot snapping bags and lifting arms,
to soft pink frosting that promises sweet taste of strawberries.

Do you ever dream into the light of me: some single shaft in autumn?
To know would make my death far away.

While you work, I sit and eat, reading *USA Today,*
but when I lift the coffee or turn the page,
I see you staring at me.
You nod and smile—what a hundred times now with all these days
when I come in to gaze:
your large brown eyes,
the darkness of your flesh,
your black hair curled,
the fine down on your arms,
the hatred that flashes from you,
your sullen wait for some command: "Two cinnamon cakes."

What pretext could I give to you,
English lessons,
some struggling conversation,
my hand would be on all your beauty?

So yesterday I tossed the small slip of paper with my name and number
over the counter.

I wager in my mind: What will happen? Did I violate some trust, frighten you?
I doubt if ever you should call,
and I am uncertain if I want you to awaken some hope, some danger,
or some love.

Today I seem content looking out the window,
with blurred images of lips and eyes;
your handsome looks from Bombay,
your staring and smiling,
how you mopped the floor
around my feet,
so that I could see the beauty lines of your slender body,
how you would not look away when I gazed into you;
and how our love making, arranged in both our minds,
was separated only by a thousand years
of language and two distant cultures,
and the greater dangers to express these desires
in this white room that floods
with the odor of frying pastries,
piety, and obesity.

In early autumn, when I inquired after you, the counter girl snapped a bag open;
"Gone to Atlanta," she said,
dropping a glazed doughnut
into the waxed white bag.

"Was there anything else you wanted?"

2002

Bucharest in the Afternoon

In my room, this easing moment holds summer filled:
Marius, in green leaves pushing against the screen—close to me;
the mowed grass of the garden enters a pungent smell,
the thigh scent of Marius I dream for—far distant is here.

He haunts me day and night in this house.
Wherever I look, in the scent of the grass,
this Corpus Christi is elbow—propped to gaze at me,
lusty-love eyes;
with nonchalance
he places his yearning between his legs,
resting a bud to me,
a given promise to all humanity.

Marius in his chat room, A4Alive
My monitor (two prison cells)
gives his perfect naked splendor.
Time is filled with this phantom and his sharing,
holy like a Sanctus bell ringing, shattering all boredom and lethargies,
to announce the wafer made body, descending,
for the feast I would consume.

In a perfection of summer,
the white moth flutters down,
like the falling of heaven's manna in wind
this consecration descends.

I breathe all in at four thirty-seven—
this moment of Marius remembering,
a peculiar touching which wants far more—
his flesh for all eternity.
We are bound in his earthly poverty and mine,
a knotting in love and lust,
no enemy or conqueror,
but creation binding, each to each,
rising from ancient dust.
Far distant, he's here.

2011

The Ohio Songbird Sings and Dances Online: Dedicated to All Real Women

I.

The gay Ohio songbird,
in Paradise town,
danced his dance,
with cardboard angel wings
chalked pink and lavender.
And I, browsing in tedium,
on a muggy afternoon
saw him twice, <u>cam 2 cam</u>,
skinny and young.
I assumed his parents gone,
so for a lark he made gay burlesque
to entertain August's lonely men.

Emerging from a far room,
frolicking down a hall,
in silk trousers and a blouse.
Purple sequins in the light,
he bowed himself to the Midwest
and dedicated his show to all "real women,"
not defined.

He danced sequences of tease and lust,
singing muffled into his mike,
then vanished down the hall to reappear
in shorts, bikinis, or Calvin Klein underwear.

Finale of it all,
he held a placard, crayon printed,
"Dedicated to all real women
in the state of Ohio."
I wondered the meaning to him
and tossed the words for sense.
But shown in reverse,

another enigma put on enigma
and unreadable;
he never knew,
nor I.

II.

But remember now not dancing but sitting
on the rocks taken from a farmer's field,
to make space for rows of green rustling corn
in the smallest wind, a stifling heat.
The house was empty.
I put the boom box on the porch to listen:
"Oh, Shenandoah, I know you're leaving."
The wistful grieving melody, up from the blue mountains,
was my yearning, remembered for the blond boy
at work in Ebelink's Green House
where jasmine bloomed in winter
and in summer became a humid jungle
of torpid desire among the golden banded lilies of Japan,
the scent stirring our sweating bodies,
the pollened stamen staining the fragile petals.

On a summer day in 1954, atop the lily house
we scrapped dried putty
from the glass and wooden frames
to be sealed and repainted.
In that afternoon, side by side,
I could see light golden hair on his arm
quiver in a small breeze,
while I feared
the love, heavy growing in my chest,
the desiring to touch what I knew forbidden,
but I would not freedom-fly from such smothering
or take what was lovely in that day.

III.

I was afraid for him, the Ohio dancing boy—some similar fate;
and wondered how long he would wait before taking flight
on angel wings of pink and lavender
or remain to sing alone and dry in the heat
among the murmuring rows of alien corn,
or nodding lilies imprisoned beneath burning glass.

I watched the boy aflame, running down the hall in rainbow shorts, akimbo wings,
and whispered,
"Abandon that house of only dreams—
take flight.
Do not be lost to tenderness and salty flesh,
etherized in lilies deceiving scent,
the beauty of desire bent;
take flight;
and I would earlier lift my hand
to what had summoned me,
from deep inside,
some yearning for a friend
some hand descending—
sparked from divine mystery within.
        To move from illusion to warm flesh,
        a sweeter scent than lilies under glass.

2001

The Chicago Guy at XXX Match.Com:

Four private photographs: a game of cards

If I were to have them in my hand with choice of only one to keep,
I would hesitate to select, but know for certain, I desired one to play.

All are in settings, but for one with only a solitary speaking face,
"I am this," it says, "and calm."
The hair slightly peaked, I see.

Then in another, he leans against a stone wall, with resting posture; silence beckons,
but eyes hidden dark beneath a knitting of black wool, pulled down.
If only I could touch the cap, would I pull it off?
What mystery to reveal of eyes, and why?
And what other things then in mischief lift,
like the sweater, open at the neck to see fair flesh?

Then to the photograph, he, a young man, in a yellow shirt,
like bright sun in a fenced garden, with white petunias,
what exact word to speak, to convince absolute the beauty of him?

And last, at the long café bar, how far would I have to lean
in pretended intention to kiss just one cheek
but stretch for more?

Only now I am certain I would all four keep and know;
to play, to win some rushing, haunting perfection of man,
with cards so well dealt.

2010

Holy Week Meditation 2010: Corpus Christi and the Washing of Feet

He came to Simon Peter, who said to him,
"Lord, are you going to wash my feet? Then wash all of my body."

Jesus said, "You do not know now what I am doing,
but later you will understand"—this parting, this last love sign, and large purpose,
cleansing the feet of men who walked on the dust—roads of Judea.

Peter, he touched your feet before his loss of flesh.
On this last night of life, Christ, with soft hands, is washing feet.
Tomorrow the nails sound, deep into flesh,
but tonight he touches your feet.

If Christ were to wash my feet, I would be redeemed,
and intimacy bonded with him, weeping—
the touch of his satisfying hand, with oil,
as Magdalena once held his in fragrance;
this Christ, anointed for living and a tomb,
caressing with her long black hair;
and Mark said, "Then the Beloved washed His feet
and knew the parting."
And I would live in the innocent fecundity of the garden,
a flesh and spirt borne to one.

Come ancient lovers: Adam, Eve
drop the fig leaves for the fire of desire
and touch of the dove-wing brushing,
spirit sent, soul crying out in pleasure,
from all eternity—God sound,
cosmic yearning, making slow all creation,
flesh to flesh: the root and bending stem
leafing to one flower.

I say, like Peter, "If you will wash my feet, wash my whole body,"
with a towel tinctured in ancient rivers flowing down from a benevolent throne;
then I will be made companion and teach your ways.
Touch me in Eucharist, together consumed.

* * *

Anthony, my hustler brother, called to my bed again.
white face on the light of night,
soft sheen like the skin of a speaking snake
to curl sensual round my cold flesh;
hard strength against my side, healing oil;
what early fathers would not allow: Christ with any man or woman,
held back from strife, joy, full flesh, then I know you would not chasten
but consent this ecstasy, denied, springing from the loins which sing
your sons and daughters to eternity.

Cling us to the first innocence, and Abel not slain, but kissed,
as we to each would be
when morning dawned the world green to perfect nakedness.
Be with us then, O Christ, pleasured pure in our bed.

* * *

On this last night of life, the word made flesh,
with soft hands, is washing feet.
Tomorrow nails sound—the corpus crushed,
but tonight from second Eden coming, the touching of flesh,
washing of feet.

2010

My Lips Are Beggars on Your Lips

Jason, my lips are beggars on your lips,
my fingers, benevolent slenderness,
to trace lace, spinning smoothness,
to lift with silken threads,
prevail and part your lips.

Once within,
my tongue will drink,
in corporal dreams,
your soul to share salt water from an ancient sea,
the slow beginning of eternal Deity.

My hands are beggars on your body,
never knocking, entering all your flesh,
consuming as the yawning mouth of darting fish,
to surface not, but feed on your body given
the veil of the temple in silence rent.

The hem-bells of the priest ring,
within the presence of divinity.

With you,
my ark and covenant,
what is forbidden,
I touch
and know invisible, made real:
Creator and creation drawn within to sip sweet wine, our salvation sealed;
and lies once pressed on me, now in lightning struck, revealed.

2012

Three Voices: Men 4 Rent, Sweet Anthony

In a photograph, his head, cocked, shows less his face,
but two blue eyes to enter through to some distant space,
away in wind, to lush fertility, this primal fragrance.

The flash of light, the curved beauty,
posted photograph of smoothness unblemished,
to be drawn to his body of milk and honey.

I come back to perfected art to touch more each part
and dream again the brushing of a hand,
the one friend descending,
the yearned for quenching.

One to complete the being of self, to make whole,
to approach the edge where life and death balance dangerously,
in rush of cosmic sacredness,
where there is no body nor separate soul,
but all is holy,
this making of love.

He slips his black shorts off
naked on my bed, already hard, thick,
like a spring branch in winter,
to shatter that long ice, the sad reading of Lorca;
what I dreamed for: nothing a sin, but love touched.

Anthony naked on my bed; the fine line of black hair
running down from his navel to the mound of hair,
to the deliciousness of fruit, as heavy laid on bended branch,
taken by the hand, devoured—his love in me;
this apple God offered, not a snake,
to know Him, equal within us.

I would end in the act of being loved by Anthony.
This myth and all rituals: his sweet tongue, lips, and hard nipples,
My body pulled close enough to pierce,
his blade cutting asunder all bound in a knot,
to be born anew as man.
What space does it enter, this leaping soul, where does it go to unleash such
fevered eagerness, to be one love, consecrated host descending?

It is the other coming in, this deep within,
this platonic soul and word becoming flesh.
I would have him rest in me into eternity, this cosmos,
the perpetual moment made from the dust of stars
into the dying stars be made dust again with him,
be eternal in this desire fulfilled,
be with the word made flesh and the flesh made word.
To rest, to sleep, flesh wings folded.

At last, I am made flesh.

2010

Byzantine Prince: Koray

My love is all time beyond the past,
even in this time ease unfolds eons ago
fulfilling this afternoon of snow:
the flakes and turning pages, to a Paterian dream:
for this past, I live to speak;
not these cold days,
winter's dark haze,
but to what I know:
illusions in words,
Keat's truth perfected and sublime,
the flesh of his beauty on the white sands of Mersin,
where we swam in fresh water,
defying the strong pull of the stream caressing, our groins and chests,
current soothing our bellies,
where the Yilgin River empties all history into the salt of the sea,
and my hands would have reached to hold the sun in him,
his eyes filled with white light, bright,
black hair heavy on his forehead,
laughing beyond the eucalyptus grove
deep into cicadas stinging song and strove
beyond to this hour of black crows, high;
cawing, cawing an echo from that yearning time:
a brush of drying sand
still clinging
on the salt-taste
of his thigh,
imagined.

2015

The Dark Gardener

He came late afternoon, heavy from the day of work,
now to plant five perennials for me: fox glove, day lily, lupine, amethyst in the snow
and phlox a deeper shade of rose than the seven planted some time past.

In the other years, I had watched him mow the grass and repair the roof,
always in summer—the only time I saw him, this bronzed man from Ecuador,
when he and I were younger—twenty-five years, I say.

Then was the same story:
he stripped to his denim shorts, his chest covered with black hair,
the work and wind quivering his flesh and fineness.
I had watched him paint the garage.

The gardener from Ecuador came now to the new house and planted,
trimmed the shrubbery and set what remains of the green wicker furniture,
to the patio—two chairs at a time above his head, the black hair of his armpits
dense; I dreamed out to the fragrance. He never looked at me.
I had thought to ask him to set up the fountain in the back,
but for my own reason said no.
My lover Jonathon had always done that until winter
and an overdose of heroin laid him dead, on a stranger's kitchen floor.

And I, not knowing if the fountain's steady streams would make more grief or less,
said no again, but looked at the water in the pond, clear to the bottom;
last summer's leaf, lay still decaying, like rusting tin.

Then went to the front of the house to see what was finished,
but mostly stood around, explained the places of plants and how short the bushes
should be trimmed, feeling my age and his youth still.

I didn't gaze hard as I sometimes did at the other place—I mean to stare
to see the mound where his cock was or linger a glance on the curls of his black hair.
He was sweating, the droplets shinning like broken glass to cut and bleed.
And I short of breath, stood around and around, not knowing what I was looking for,
not of this time or place. But in the end, the fountain was set,
the bronze boy with his arms open wide to all that Is: the Embracer of Life.

I saw what had returned from winter: the hastes and wild wood fern,
one sending sharp spears up from the earth, the other unfurling a green lace;
I went to him in mind and earlier time: the fountain dripping water
beneath the bronze boy sitting on the bronze pomegranate,
the patina of winter having turned them green; water fell short steady notes.

And the dark gardener, unsummoned, comforter and healer,
went about his priestly tasks, not knowing the vastness of his restoration,
the settling of strife, returning splendor in the seasons of a year:
soft tearing the veil from top to bottom, spilled fertility and holiness out.
Placing all in order for the birth of spring and summer, a new time growing,
drawing what was past into this season.

2004

The Hustler's Love: A Perfection of Sacred Lust to Stillness Quieting

Bent with sleep,
the night heavy with snow on branches,
wind pushing off the mounds,
in silence crashing on limbs beneath,
here and far away,
they fell fast in freezing mist.

Awake to all of the darkness in a silent house,
with Jason's calm breathing,
I stood at the window,
beneath, a single deer lay sleeping,
naked, looking out at whiteness,
caught in the whim of the wind, to slant, to swirl,
the sky a dark line of blue.
"Christ, it is beautiful,"
not a mark of boot or hoof, only the smooth spreading out of flakes,
and I aware in the bed of Jason's nakedness, given;
our seeking, in the other, passion's heat,
on January's winter night,
woods hushed in snow;
wind murmuring intimate perfections.

Near—away, deep night fell me into sleep,
his breathing, a constant spirit on my face,
made all the house in silence,
keeping.

2010

The Desired Boys of Summer and the Innocence of My Childhood Gazing

1967, Grand Rapids:

(The horny boys of summer,
youthful Apollonian males of this pious city,
naked in their beds,
beneath white Jockeys and the light blue cotton spread
with white sailboats and red banners printed,
"In ecstasy I call his name,
shooting warm semen,
into tissues
of White Clouds,
drifting out to Reed's Lake":
the clever student at South High School had written in his journal)

* * *

1948, Bridgeman:

Shirtless, bronzed bodies of youth,
place of my childhood and early dreams,
where I sat beneath the honeysuckle,
on a fallen tree inhabited by the little people
who also appeared in the funny papers
and with whom I talked;
then before the war, the high school boys played basketball in fading afternoons
of late August, when autumn, the last before the war, cooled them,
the heat of their game arousing other passions,
with the sun on gyrating games,
teasing each other's mouths
and eyes,
fast legs in the dust,
quick turns
and made me laugh,
fooling each other
and into greater deceptions they played—or I alone, a child;
what did the blonde beauty keep from the others,
while adolescent groins stirred

and from the dark patches of hair beneath his arms
fecundity,
in spice sweat,
scented soft in sunset,
with my tongue against his flesh—
that child was such a dreamer,
drifting out from Michigan's shores
with his green boat to escape desire,
or seek it more in some distant place;
all invented and accomplished.

He would go there some day,
to the shining domed city,
Byzantium.
He had seen the picture in the black book,
Journeys Through Bookland:
a many decked ship with golden sails
would take him there.

1970

Image: Vision of a Soul

Photograph # 1

What are you but dark brown curves to undulate, now fixed:
your head, your hair swept elegant to round and round,
you shoulder smooth in sheen
beneath the strap of pulled-up shirt
to show what of you, but warm flesh, lean
and draped gold chain to reflect some flame against your neck,
to pull nipples tight against your chest.

Your navel sunk in shadowed skin,
your slipping shorts to show a crescent ass ascending.

You stare into your pod, as if you seek some sacred message
written to affirm your being, hope, desires.

All held above far spreading fingers:
Creator's making.

2016

VI

TWO POETS

Little Ashes of Lorca in the Wind

In the film *Little Ashes,* we hear Salvador say, "Lorca, you are this painting.
And eighty years from now you will still live."
"Oh no," the voice answered, "I will only be a ghost,
and I don't want to be a ghost,
but write my name on the painting,
and my little ashes will live forever."

At the theater, Dali's mouth had laughed at the puppet: a priest fornicating.
Lorca desired the lips of the laughing painter.
He watched his mouth drink from the bottle of wine:
lips pursed, curled, separated, laughed, and laughed harder.

In the phosphorus of night, they swam in the sea, the black water turning blue,
legs and arms moved light as cork, an ancient dance:
twisting, and spreading, delicate curves, making trails of light, phosphorous- silver,
even held in the droplets falling.

Consumed with desire,
man swam toward the other,
treading water—
dark eyes gazed,
then lips closed on salty lips,
long lusted in love, but hidden;
now opened the mouth of death.

In Andalusia, near Granada, the city of gypsies singing,
Franco's Civil Guard chose an olive grove in heavy blossom for murder.
The poet's voice for the republic, for freedom,
and kisses became his misfortune in a field of whispering and curses: *faggot.*
The blindfold opened to thirteen rifles.

He listening for the blowing of ashes,
long enough for us to see the butt of a rifle
had slashed his lips open,
death's kiss, marked with blood, dried black—
the trembling crescendo at the edge of life and death: *duende.*

Thirteen shots, one more, and the mouth of death devoured
the mouth of the poet,
who whispered in the wind the songs of gypsies.

2010

Deep Song for Lorca

I hear the gypsies sing
that Lorca loved.

What suffering in Spain the gypsies knew,
what death the gypsies knew,
what dark blood spilling out
and coins from a glass jar,
and Lorca
standing in a field
of wind whispered songs,
the sharp splitting of a fascist shot,
this killing of gypsies and Lorca's lip split open.

The dragon by the side of the road devoured singers and a poet.

Sing gypsies, sing,
draw your voice
that Lorca loved,
sing "Conte Jondo,"
the long, trilling notes
of pain and love,
from deep within
the cold waters
of Fuente Grande,
the Moors bubbling tears,
that Lorca knew,
long shadows of Andalusia
Lorca knew.

Sing the silence of Lorca.

2010

Looking at a Photograph of Constantine Cavafy at Seventeen Years of Age in 1880

I moved the photograph of Constantine Cavafy
to the oak pedestal between the desk and the French doors,
to eliminate the reflection of my lamp in the glass of the frame;
but now, when I bend forward to see more fully the darkness of his youth:
full curl of black hair, curve of lips, soft light on the smooth left cheek,
the other in mysterious shadow,
my aging face is reflected back from the glass,
as if we were once together in early dusk of Constantinople.

His eyes look to his left, to the man walking in the park, I imagine.
We both are stunned by the beauty of our sensuous phantoms.

The body of the poet buried in the Greek cemetery was not the form
of this Hellenistic loveliness, long fled.
I, with these years, could not allure so fair a young man.

The ancient Greeks, living again in his poetry, have names long forgotten:
Dimitris, who shed so quickly his kingly robes, and Patroklos
whose death made Achilles horses weep.
The turn of fate undid them—lost in their own time,
now drawn back into Cavafy's sonnets.

The young men of Alexandria from the tavernas, parks,
reflected in a shop window beckoned once to Cavafy—all remain nameless.
They vanished out of Cavafy's life—
all turned away from the late night glass
long before he wrote their passionate encounters:
behind shutters, in the shadows of empty streets—
his own bed, only a few times.
Those handsome men Cavafy touched in eager heat and frantic fear,
fumbling to pull open the shirt to desired flesh—
now that lust is the cold of a moonless night.
And he too in his grave fifteen years
before his poetry was gathered—
unaware of fame to disturb him in his silent reveries kept only for himself,
and in poetry these impassioned specters summoned back in the night,
in words, an evidence of having been.

The flesh of the men once nodding to him were taken with him
into the parted waves of time, unnamed, unknown,
like the ancient Greek men fallen back into eons ago.

When he left his rooms in Alexandria for the last time, the cancer muting his sonorous voice,
he carried all the possessions of his life and two folders of poetry in a suitcase.
He said to a friend, "This is the same suitcase I brought with me, to this place, in my youth; I bought it one night in a hurry to go to Cairo for pleasure."

So the words were the last sounding of his voice in the small rooms
and the beginning of his exile from Alexandria
to death, the great silence.

The reflections in the glass have vanished,
as if they had never been.

May 9, 2009

VII

TURKEY

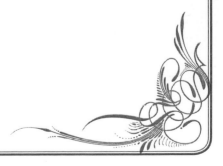

Reflections on Istanbul Rising from the Sea, A Half Century Later

This afternoon, a lazy overlay of images from other centuries,
increase to blended colors:
the towers, rounded domes,
crescent moons, fallen from the sky,
a clear vision
of fragmented rays:
tiles of terra-cotta clay,
slant against the cobalt sea
flickering, diming,
measuring an eternity of sinking suns,
on vast civilizations, Constantine undone,
but art remains a history and stands.

* * *

In my youth, the *San Marco* sailed across the Marmara Sea,
up from the Corinth Canal and Dardanelles.

From a light mist, Istanbul began to rise:
Topkapi, the cone chimneys;
then as if sinking still into the earth from heaven made,
Sultan Ahmet Mosque and Holy Wisdom rose up,
whispering each to each their mysteries.

Nearer distance held towers, palaces, mosques, and minarets,
a brush of lighted copper had tinted all.
This Istanbul and Byzantium—glowed full in the city.
Yeats knew well that place to which all poets go to learn their art,
to make the harp
through which the winds of civilizations blow.

Istanbul is still a coppered sun when I dream the *San Marco* sails me there.

March 25, 2010

The *Anadoğlu Express*

I remember the loveliness of trains while I was in Turkey during the early sixties. Even before my adventures in Turkey, trains had been a part of my life. My father was a signal maintainer for the Pere Marquette Railroad; he made trains present in the life of my brother and me. He talked about faraway places, and I remember as a child standing between two ribbons of silver blue track, stretching beyond the town, narrowing, finally merging on the other side of the woods. I was "standing on the tracks" as I looked down them. I thought that they went forever and ultimately led to great adventure, even beyond my child's imagination.

What I dreamed that day in rural Michigan was true; the trains I have ridden have brought me great visions, enabled me to stand next to beautiful people, and, importantly, to see other than myself, to see cultures other than my own. Difference was a gift to be received and respected—a part of the awe of existence.

As I begin to write about the *Anadoğlu Express* and think back to those times, I am a little sad, realizing that time is finished and the great wheel cannot be turned back. In my life, I have accomplished degrees, friends, homes, a college teaching career, a parish church, and lovers; I am grateful. But nothing has surpassed the splendor of my youth and the fast pace of my walk, jumping to land on the deck of the still approaching ferry that would take me up the Bosporus. Why was this far-off place, this foreign land so full of wonder and happiness for me? It was the fulfillment of dreams, romance, the sound of the horn of a large ship, moving out to the Marmara Sea—it was my youth, in a far place on the Anatolian plains, near Caesarea of Cappadocia, the village of Talas, and the school of Turkish youth, high on a cliff.

But I am sure that the trains, the great Wagon Lit Expresses, as I knew them, no longer exist. That the names have changed, the schedules have changed, and in Turkey, as in America, the diesel has replaced the steam engine: the shrill whistle in the dark night is silent, a ghost passing those remote villages with their rows of poplar trees in the light of a waxing moon.

I would assume that the great Wagon Lit Coaches have been backed into a railyard, some place distant, from where they once departed to Ankara, Adana, Istanbul, and Izmir. If I could find the coach that I rode in, on the Istanbul Express, a great deluxe train that left Ankara at 8:00 PM and find the first from which I stared out into the night, before walking down to the dining car where the butter, like small seashells on ice was served—that great train which in the morning before arriving at Haydar Pasha Station would pass along the Marmara Sea; certainly, I would go to it. I would walk through the dirty yards, stared at as strange by the men working, and I would board the coach and walk down the aisle and sit in the compartment, remembering the jolts, the rhythm, the clusters of small town children, the railroad station cafes, and the hard butter shell melting on the toast. I would put my hand on the plush seat, touching something real that existed beyond the memory—the actual remnant.

My old friend Dorothy Stephens warned me about going back to Turkey for fear that I would only know pain and grief, but I went. I have always gone. I have stood in a garden where I desired the lips of my lover who has been dead these thirty years; I have seen the same orange poppies again decades later.

Everything is transient in life, and it seems that our living simply takes us to an end, a grave, and of course, in that place, all is irrevocably lost, certainly ourselves, as we have known our faces and hands. We may remain a memory for some, for a time, but eventually, that too will end. And the child will look at the same name as his own on the stone and say to his father, "Who was that?" and the father will say, "I don't know, someone in the family." But the child will never know about the desired kiss, never taken in the garden while the sun, in haze, set over the city of Kayseri, or have described the fleeting visions of the Marmara Sea, in early morning on the Istanbul Express.

* * *

I had been sailing on the *Umit,* once a sponge boat, then converted into a sailboat with a motor. I went with Mary Lou and some of her women friends. The sailing had been an unexpected part of my return to Turkey, and before leaving America, I had planned on spending a week in the interior. After five days on the *Umit,* I had to leave. Mary Lou did not want to take the sailboat back to Bodrum where I could have easily made connections to Ankara; instead, she made arrangements for a boy to walk with me from the coast to the first village that we would find— the village was Taslica, meaning with stones or stony. Two handsome young Turks drove me over to Mulga where I spent the night at the bus driver's house. In the morning, we drove to Dalaman, which was a three-hour trip through the mountains. Although I had been worried about missing my flight to Ankara, via Istanbul, I made the flight. The flight had originated in Cyprus, and when it landed, it blew a tire. I was trying to take a picture of the plane, but the military police would not let me. A mustache scissors was removed from my carry-on luggage, but it was returned to me in Istanbul. I remember there was a system for loading the baggage. After we checked our bags, at boarding time, we had to go out to the tarmac to point to our suitcase. Then it was loaded into the hold when we got on the plane—a protection against bombs being planted in luggage and then the passenger not taking the flight. If you didn't point to your bag, it was not loaded onto the plane. I understood the instructions that were given in Turkish. But there were tourists who did not understand and thought that their luggage was in the process of being loaded. Just before the doors were closed, there was an announcement in Turkish that several passengers had not claimed their luggage. But no one stirred. As we began to taxi away, I looked down and saw suitcases standing on the tarmac. I could imagine the great confusion for those tourists. And I would surmise that it would have been very complicated retrieving the luggage.

I had a layover in Istanbul; then I flew on to Ankara. The Turkish Airlines bus on the way into the city of Ankara stops at the Central Railroad Station. There was a train leaving in just twenty minutes for Kayseri. Its final destination was Aleppo, Syria. When I got on, I saw the train was crowded. There were not enough seats for everyone.

A village woman, with the traditional full pants and colorful prints, sat on the aisle floor with many packages and baskets, talking to herself, a chicken was in one of the baskets. The coaches all had compartments, and the aisle ran down one side of the coach. I panicked for a moment. I did not want to stand for seven hours. I stood in the aisle amid the chaos. The revolutions increased on the diesel locomotive, and the train, around eight o'clock, began to move out. There is a point, going through the yards, when a loud gong suddenly sounds. I had forgotten about it until I heard it then, again for the first time in years. Usually, when I traveled between Kayseri and Ankara, I had a seat on the fast express or an entire compartment to myself on the regular express, and I would hear the gong and look up from my reading and know that we were well under way; we would cross the bridge over Attaturk Boulevard, not far from a charming hotel where I had stayed many times.

I remember that Carol and Huldah stayed there once. And I, on one of my visits, was able to get a corner room on the fourth floor, which gave me a good view down the boulevard.

Now standing leaning out the window, hearing the gong, memories overtook me. I was in two different times, the exciting present: colorful peasants, the happiness of the travelers, and the beginning of the rhythmic motion of the train, which rocked me happy and then gently pushed me against the wall of the aisle, constantly changing my perspective, showing me something new—a distant bridge, a section of highway.

Then there was the distant past and a clear remembrance of the many trips I had made across the Anatolian plains; and one exact trip I had made on the Motorlu train, the fast three car express, the pride of Turkish Railroads, when I was going to Adana and on to Tarsus for a conference at St. Paul's College. On that trip, I marveled at the large beauty of the Anatolian plains and the constant appearing and disappearing of Mount Ergyus, snowcapped against the deep blue of the sky, rising out of the burned plains. First, the mountain would be at the head of the coach on my left, then slip by to the last window, and then be gone only to reappear on my right. I was excited. I knew and loved the beauty of the plains, the drying wheat had been the bread of the Roman Empire.

Now years after that journey, I was going back to Kayseri on an overnight mail train with hundreds of happy people leaning out the windows, into the last light of the dull orange sun, sinking through the dust to the distant horizon, the heat of the earth vanishing as purple shadows formed, stretching out long from rows of poplars. I righted myself and leaned out the window, and the fragrance of the dry stubble cooling and taking in the moisture of the early evening moved into my being.

Fifteen minutes after we left Ankara, I walked the entire length of the train to see if there were any seats; there weren't any. I went to the dining car, and there was a table that was vacant. All the occupants in the car were men, most of whom were drinking beer. I ordered too much food. I had thought that each item on the menu was a la carte, not knowing that each item was a complete dinner. So I wound up with three dinners. I had noticed a table of three young men just to my left who were rowdy. I attributed it to the beer, already six empties on the table. They called the waiter over and began an argument, with much noise and many gestures. Then one of them came over to my table and spoke to me in simple English. They wanted to know if I would join them. They had argued with the waiter about the amount of food he had brought me. In Turkish, they said,. "Why did you bring him all of that food? Why didn't you explain to him that each item was a complete dinner?"

The waiter responded, "I thought he wanted all the food."

I was satisfied and mellowed with the good food. I was happy, and after three days of silence, here were three people who were patient and willing to talk with me in my limited Turkish and their limited English. They had explained to me that they had been in Ankara for a long weekend of sex and drinking—loose living—and that they came from a small village called Sherifli, meaning with "honor." After talking and drinking, we came to a tired, relaxed sense of one another, and there were comfortable silences, interrupted eventually with some question or some new information. We had become friends. They had helped a young American—they had been kind to me in my need. We were knowing one another with ease.

Eventually, we walked back to where I had been standing in the aisle, and there began a constant moving against one another in the sudden lurching movements, violent swaying, and quick reductions in speed. The four of us were holding on to two leather straps or, from time to time, grabbing hold of a chrome bar next to the window, when there was a more violent movement in the train. As we held the straps, our bodies moved lightly against one another, then forcibly. We swayed around and around, brushing lightly a chest, a stomach, a thigh. And when a sudden lunge threw us off balance, we all reached for the chrome bar, sometimes our hands falling upon other hands or a hand would open and take hold of another and with a strong, pull toward the man, steadying the other. Sometimes we did not let go of the hand. We were comfortable in our silence and comfortable and brave in our not planned deception of those around us. From time to time, I would put my head out the open window and feel the rush of cool air, breathe in the sweet odors that come up only from the Anatolian plains in the dead of summer nights. There was no sense of a sexual urgency. I was aware of a quiet desire that would not be fulfilled. It didn't need to be. After the constant worry about plane and train connections, the long day—that time with the young Turks, swaying in many fragrances from the plains and the men, almost always all of us with our eyes closed—is the recollection of a profound intimacy and love, comfort and peace. We were exhausted and rested against one another—a kind affection of the intensities of our days.

Their journey was not as long as mine, and eventually, we came to Sherifli. The train slowed and stopped. We all lost our balance into one another and this time were brave enough let fall our hands. No one would have suspected anything but four young men losing their balance. When I looked out the window, at first I saw only blackness. Then I saw the one bright lamp, the only light in the village. And I knew to where we had come. One of those small villages where the train usually does not stop but speeds past on its way to some other important place. We had been near the end of the coach, and their departure was sudden. I think that the train was not in Sherifli for more than thirty seconds. One of the men, before leaving, had gone earlier to several compartments, looking for a seat for me. He finally bought me a seat, which he showed me, and I went there after they had left. But I didn't stay. I walked back to the place where we had stood as friends and opened to one another. I clung to one of the straps for the next three hours. It was an easy journey—I had not been alone.

That night, there was no rush of nostalgia, no regret for not having dared more. What would have been the meaning of our having exchanged addresses. They had come into my life for those few hours. I would always remember with a deep affection, the warmth of their bodies against me, and our warm breathing on soft necks and faces. The strange mingling of our flesh. The comfort we were to one another that night of early boisterous conversation that for an hour fell so silent, swaying in the dim light, never to happen again.

In two hours, while the night was still black, we pulled into Bogazici to transfer to the waiting shuttle train. For the first time in many years, I stood watching the breathing of a steam locomotive, the stuttering sounds, the hiss, the rush of air out of the stack; passengers were leaving the shuttle to board the express that would continue on to Aleppo. There was an American couple who did not understand that they were to leave the shuttle and board the express. I helped them and then boarded the shuttle that would take me back to Kayseri. The journey was a short one. I leaned out the window and listened to the power of the engine. Such an engine had pulled the Istanbul Express; the most beautiful of trains, which had taken me away from Marjorie, and the Ankara Express, which had taken me away from Gerrard. He had stood outside my compartment window; suddenly, the train had lurched, and a large cloud of steam enveloped him. When it cleared, he was gone. We had made love that summer. These steam engines had taken me to different destinies.

In Kayseri, I left the train and stood on the platform; people rushed past me, and soon I was standing alone. The station emerged a dark silhouette against a sky, which had lightened to a hint of gray with the beginning of three ribbons of gold silk.

This was the place where Umit Bey, the school secretary, saw the small—perhaps all—the students off to their homes at holiday times. His task was to be sure that the boys were on the right trains. I, myself, would sometimes be there, waiting to board the fast express for Ankara and a long weekend. I would stand amid the cries, shouts of voices, and Umit Bey's resolute response. For a moment, I could hear the wonderful pandemonium, then silence. For several minutes, I stared at the Byzantine outline of the station. Just the shape of it against the lightening sky evoked names and faces I had forgotten.

Now I wondered what I was trying to do making this long pilgrimage. I think that I was returning not to a people who were a part of my life and to place where I had lived before. One can love a place, a garden, a stand of trees, an old Greek church now abandoned, a view of the far off mountains. And I know that in that place I had had friends, a significant work, good students, and I fell in love many times. I think that when I am actually in the garden of Talas, I am marveling at beauty, creation, this thing called life, existence, itself, and my good fortune, the incredible good fortune I have had. How my days fall out good! In all the time that I have been in Turkey, there is no place to which I do not hold fast; there is the remembrance of no face that was not friendly. Some say that I live in the past. But that is not true. I think I live in the all the time of my life. The past is gone. It can only be remembered. I think that it is possible for imprints to form on the brain from which we cannot escape. So on a cool day in June, here in Michigan, when there is no cloud in the sky and there is no humidity, I will feel that I am in Talas; I know that I am not there, but the stone walks, the sound of water running, gurgling in the sluices that is there, Solmaz coming out to the veranda with fresh lemonade, the sudden flight of a black bird with white wings that is there in the mind, it cannot be erased, and when the soul decides that the mind should give it food to live on, the mind must return the images of the past that were the soul's greatest delight. When I was innocent.

Later, as I walked toward the center of the city, a young man—I would say seventeen—spoke to me in English. "Can I help you?"

I now felt fiercely independent and all this journey was mine. "No, I am just walking to the center of the city."

"Are you an American?"

"Yes."

"Are you a tourist?"

"No, I was a teacher here at Talas American School."

He paused. "I know Talas. My parents have a summer house there."

He was dressed in a military uniform. I thought he must be attending a private school. "I will be all right. I want to go to the Hitaap Hotel. I can find it."

"Yes, but I must tell you that you are walking in the wrong direction."

I laughed. "You know, I would like it if you would give some help. If you are free at this time, help me."

The dawn was breaking. The sky was streaked with flames of orange. The city glowed a soft pink. He was crisp. I never asked why he was up so early in the morning. Perhaps he had been on the train too. I listened to him talk about school, the changes in Kayseri, the uncle in his family who had gone to Robert College in Istanbul. "Yes," I would say. He stayed with me. He made the arrangements for me at the hotel. And turning from the desk, walking toward me, I could see his slender handsomeness, the beauty of his face, and always the dark brown eyes. He spoke. "Do you want me to come back for you this afternoon, or shall I wait until tomorrow morning? I will take you back to Talas. I can be your translator."

Now I know that his picture is someplace in this room. It is in a drawer, box, or album. I must see his face again. Later, I struggle to keep writing. I would rather dream and stare out the window at the green locust leaves, moving in the wind, returning sounds and faces to me. But in the silent dreaming, the text appears, and my fingers move quickly across the keys again.

I agreed for tomorrow. It would give me a day of rest, a chance to walk around the city of Kayseri again. He reminded me of one of my students in Talas: Ibrahim, whom I saw later in Istanbul, looking very much as he had in third class. I was glad that Ahmet would help me. My Turkish was not good,; and I would be able to ask the questions and say the words I wanted to say.

The next day, he did the perfect thing. He knew where the bus to Talas stopped in Kayseri, and we would take that. I bought several tokens on which are stamped "Talas Autobuserli?" I keep one of the tokens today on the shelf beneath the crucifix in my bedroom. Then we were off, Mount Ergyus on the right, the snow on the crest bright in the June morning. And stretching out from the foot hills of the mountain to the road where our bus roared on was a vastness of green, orchards and grass that had not yet been burned in the sun. Our conversation now was easy.

"Look," he said, "at the boy with the stubborn donkey. Is this how you remember Kayseri?"

"Yes, donkeys, yes, I remember the sound of donkeys."

I thought once there was an airfield over there, but now it has been moved. Marjorie and I had danced at a ball held in one of the hangers there. The evening had ended with Marjorie losing her perfume *Fem* and the two of us watching a belly dance. Huldah, the librarian, had come with us.

"Yes, it is much the same. I went to an air force ball there one time." I could smell the sweat that mingled with the dark patches of hair under his arms—this was Turkey. I had been here before. The scent did not bother me. I liked it. It was the smell of a man, not spice, not flowers, not lemon, but the smell of a virile young man whose culture I loved and respected. There always must be that look, the glance that lingers, the eyes that do not turn away but speak a desire, likeliness, and then when the bus turns and we lean thigh to thigh, arm to arm – a ride to Talas—then the moment changes, the awareness vanishes.

I was going to see the place of the ghosts that I had once loved, and I would be faithful to them. As we entered the lower village, I was totally alive. I recognized the cemetery, the mosque, and the grocery store. We could stay on the bus to go to upper Talas—the village rises, shoots up along a steep hill and cliff. But I wanted to walk the rest of the way, even though it meant climbing up the stone road in the sun. I wanted to see Wingate Hall slowly reveal itself, each new vision of it awakening: the large bell that summoned for dinner, for study session, for the Saturday ceremony in the garden by the statue of Ataturk; the room where I met the third class and where I had first seen Koray, leaning forward in the first row, and from which I had seen the crooked chimney on the *kiosk*—my one-room office from which there was the best view of the plains and where I sat reading papers and watching the slow-moving patterns of cloud-shadow across the wide plains and the *Yilanli* mountains.

And now nothing more will come to me or too much comes to me. I must stop to decide which incident I will consider, which room, and on what day and year did that happen. For I am constantly trying to sort all this time out and to put it in order. The chronology is important to me. I was once very unhappy to discover that a story that I had been telling and introducing by saying "the fall of 1962" was out of place; Marjorie had come in 1963, that had been the year that we bought the horses: *Sabah* and *Cesur.*

Ahmet and I climbed the stairs, up to the higher campus—147 steps; the students had counted them and the number was published in the year book. Sometimes, when I had counted them, I did get that number. We climbed the steps, Ahmet and I.

The next day, he met me again at the hotel, took the bus back to Talas. We went to his parents' summer home. It was very modern, had vineyards and orchards, gardens, and arbors. It was beautiful. We had lunch and walked through the land.

I made no overture to him. The time with him was a private intimacy of loveliness— that was not what the experience was. A second gift to me. Andre Gide wrote that sometimes one finds the most intense love with a stranger; it seems it would be absolute fulfillment. And one must not possess that love but keep the memory of intense desire through the remainder of life. But it was not that kind of experience. It was being humbled by the large generosity of a young man to a stranger.

I sent him a thank you card with a Japanese cutout of a bowl of flowers, very fine and detailed. He wrote back a message and thanked me for the "delicate card."

All the time had been delicate like the moment in *Ode on a Grecian Urn,* the moment of intense bond to last eternally—the ultimate Romanticism and perhaps paralysis, the perpetual postponement or perhaps just the embracing of kindness.

1968

Looking at a Photograph of Ali in 1981

He was an artist who painted in my rooms at Talas in 1963
while I watched his handsome hands and face.
The canvas was finished. I don't know what has become of it.
The photograph remains, always, some place in this house, tucked between two books,
to be rediscovered, by chance, from year to year, the autumns blowing past or
in time freezing on a January day, to stir up the disbelief it was,
to doubt such existence was, the melancholy, galloping up the high rising dirt road,
heading to the East and the snow winds, clean from the mountains.

* * *

Today, in this photograph, I see him in the school garden,
leaning against an acacia tree, full of clean lemon scent but sweeter.
Those late May flowers in Talas are still blooming. I have seen them.

He stands on a piece of curbing, separating grass from a flower bed,
but none grow in the dusty soil.
The left foot is in front of the right—he is a calm balance
in which exists no sense of the long distance ahead for him.
He is in that time, even today in my rooms,
he remains in a garden, a perfect stasis,
not knowing the morning sun, casting light on him to perfection,
will rise to noon and then begin to fall, setting beyond the purple Yilanli mountains,
making haze over the city of Kayseri, glow like apocalyptic fire,
or fear his being in this place will only fade to black and white—
some shades of gray within my walls,
in this empty vastness—
an emblem of lust and quieted love,
his and mine never vanishing.

He wears a sweater with a broad geometric pattern;
around his waist the band is plain.
Beneath the sweater are a plaid shirt and the knot of a tie at the buttoned neck.
His slacks have no press, his thumbs catch in the pockets,
so that the fingers and hands rest beneath his hips,
giving the figure a jauntiness.
The right leg is bent at the knee,
giving the body an easy lean against the tree.

His face is tilted downward a few degrees; he smiles slightly.
The moistness of his lips reflects the sun.
His eyes like brown almonds—almost lost in shadow,
but if I turn the picture to the window,
I can see them soft, obliging the photographer,
or anyone who would gaze, a gentle consent to behold the splendor
of a single moment on the Anatolian plains,
in the sound of the muezzin, calling out to prayer,
an alien voice, high haunting.

Behind him the acacia branches lace out flat against the sky—
the tops of trees growing in the vineyards below, hold all of him.
He stands in light;
no shadow has touched him, nor my hand in that green place of fecundity.
His radiance signs my salvation in the beauty of his flesh,
wrought down to earth in gentleness, created to loveliness,
a Turkish Antinous in the old school garden.

1975.

Ten Minarets at Night: Last Visit

In 1961, I sailed on the SS *Independence* from New York to Naples and continued to Istanbul on the SS *San Marco*.

One hour out of New York, I stood at the stern of the ship looking at the white wake, churning distances out of place. A voice beside me said,
"That is the way back."
"Yes, but it is vanishing."

I didn't stand long looking at the watery road back. I was young. The dream of my youth was coming about. My nostalgia is not so much of my childhood, which was comfortable and free. The church of my childhood and youth had been a heavy oppression, but that was lifted—I was free. My nostalgia is of that time in my youth when I lived in Turkey and Spain—and all became new.

So I began my sojourn from the heart of the Midwest to the Middle East. Although after four years I came back to America, I never really returned. My life here has seemed uprooted from Ancient Caesarea, the land of the early church fathers and the caves of early Christians, the mosques, the spice bazaar, the three years at Talas School and one year at Tarsus College.

Despite the past horrors, during the time of the deportation and killing of Greeks and Armenians, in Talas and surrounding villages, there was in the 1960s a peace. It must have been a place of anguish, like all places in the world where civilizations and religions have come and gone in great violence and blood, certainly even in my own country where the land was taken away from another race and religion.

I kept listening for something of long ago, but the blood of wars and massacres settles down deep in the earth, not speaking again. The sun vanished the shadows on the mountains; I thought it was a new time, and the past had not existed—so great an innocence and naiveté.

In Talas, it was only the vastness of the silent land that spoke, sometimes a braying donkey or an oxcart, perhaps two or three times a day a diesel truck or bus grinding up hill to some distant village—chickens in the morning and far away barking dogs in the night.

The soft colors of lavender, ripened wheat and light grays, shades that configured out to the horizon, eventually lost behind the mountains of the West and the diminished sun. The colors and shape of the land was the source of the silence, with the haze that hung above the city of Kayseri.

Talas was a place where I could stand on the veranda of Wingate Hall and look out in amazement at space, where the histories of people were dispersed to an echoing silence. Sometimes it is impossible for me to turn away from the inner vision of it, and I stay staring at last summer's ferns on my veranda and deep into the woods, but see only now the other place.

In Talas, I taught English language, along with some reading of short stories and novels; and I lived in a community of about twenty Americans. All my students were Turkish, a few Armenians, and were intelligent boys and young men, who studied with great energy and slept in unheated dormitories.

Years later, in 1995, on the occasion of a reunion with former American teachers and Turkish students, I arrived in Talas around noon, exhausted from the four different flights and the night lay over in Istanbul.

Hilmi, who had picked me up at the Kayseri airport, said he would leave me to rest until dinner.

I was given my old rooms, at the school, in what was then called the New Dorm, although it was an old stone dormitory with pillars and a balcony—four stories high. The three rooms I had, had shrunk into two; the room at the south end now was joined to another apartment. Hilmi helped me carry up the luggage. Then suddenly, I was left alone in the old rooms, with the door closed to the outer hallway.

I walked out onto the balcony, opening the heavy, wooden, French doors, and saw still in place the glass doors that Gerrard had had made for me in the shop on the upper campus; the glass in one of the doors was broken. With the large wooden doors open, light filled the room. The smell of the room was the same, the dampness of the plaster and the oil that was poured on the wooden floors to keep the dust down remained.

I sat In one of the chairs at the back wall of the central room and looked into the canopies of the trees. It was the same these years later as it had been when I first arrived, but a large void hung about the place—the sense of death and ruin.

How the mind evokes a gradual settling back into a place, which at first is resisted, is a mystery. The return is abrasive, but the shadows on the wall, the door frames, the alignment of the bedroom door with the window, the crow of a rooster, bring about an old reality. Is it the mind? The being warps and then settles into the new moment, which becomes the past. And I have discovered, the past sometimes steals and settles into the present, catching one unaware. So time flows backward and forward. But there is really only one time, one moment. And however close the past seems with its reality in the length of eternity, it does not reappear.

In the early 1960s, I had a small garden on the balcony, with tall oleanders. They blossomed in lavender, among the pots of red and white germaniums and the small pool of water in a large piece of concrete. In my room on the north wall was a large wooden crucifix that I had bought in Palma Majorca. In the late afternoon, the oleander branches would make dancing patterns on the wall and crucifix, even caressing the corpus of Christ. The memory of that room and time still tease and torment me; the time never to be retrieved.

Svetlana Boym writes about such moments—nostalgia, as an idyllic time of longing for a place in time that is gone but which can be recollected at will and longed for and may be a comfort in what is unbearable loss in life, which might prevent the fulfilling of life in the present.

In Talas, all was the same: the clarity of the air on the Anatolian plains, the pungent odors of foliage and burned grass in the air, the distant barking of a dog, and the feeling that some great event was about to occur; all was the same, except all past life was irrevocably changed. No friends would ever return, no lesson taught. In the end, one must say, "He is gone, dead. That time is over—it was a different life."

Later that afternoon, I climbed the 147 steps to the upper campus and rested in the children's cemetery: The colors of the mountains in the distance were yellow and lavender, and the village of Talas, with crumbled Armenian walls was below; dry grass beneath my feet, and the lilac bush covered with small seed pods. Near the gray stones of graves were the same bending poppies. Looking toward the house, large Wingate Hall, my eyes searched past the gardens and the acacia trees; and for a moment in my imagination all time was suspended.

What time was it? Could I call out a name and expect an answer? I did not call out. But something inside struggled to regulate the time; and to comprehend why what seems present is not although the body and mind perceive in that other time, granting a peace and madness, and I say something like it all comes back to me. For some, the return is a great sorrow, for some a great sorrow and joy. For none, is it only a great joy. Some would ask me the disturbing question, the baffling question, "Then why return at all—particularly alone?"

I had many conversations with the boys, now men, who had come back for the reunion, dinner in the chill of the night air half way up Mount Erciyes, watching the lights of the city, the same shimmering silver dots, flickering; and I all the time transfixed, as if looking into the holy of holies.

When all the people had left, I stayed on an extra night. But as soon as I walked to the upper campus, I knew that the place was no longer mine. The workers for the university were there, most of them just watchmen with their families, eating the meat they had cooked over the outdoor fire.

When I had talked with some of the children and men, all was finished, and I could be alone again. I sat in a place where I had never sat before, at the north end of the upper campus; it was a place for the students to play; they were very good at tossing out paper airplanes that shot out high over the drying vine yards below. From that soil mixed with volcanic ash, hardened, exists a view on three sides, stretching to the far mountains, a sense of space and great land, once an ancient caravan route from Bagdad to Byzantium.

It was dark, and I sat staring once again at the lights of Kayseri. I realized there have been places in my life where vision extended beyond any mundane comprehensions, on to the endlessness of the round earth, the largeness of creation the Cosmos and history, and in that moment, I flew into it, like the Hindu god Garuda who is free to fly beyond the border of non-ending space beyond the firmament. Garuda returns with his long beak to destroy evil on the earth. I want never to return, forever changed in wonder by what is beyond the human mind—no word in language catches that vision. Like those mystical saints, one remains still and breathes silently.

Talas was one such place, among others were the Bay of Izmir, the small plaza at the end of Calle Tur in Ibiza in the Balearic Islands, the towers of the Church of the Holy Family in Barcelona. From the windows of my first apartment on the fourth floor of the "new dorm, I could see the lights of Kayseri. And the day in the sun, passing overhead, was constantly changing the colors and shapes of the plains, making them shine, throwing great shadows, creating purple, and the soft end of day in coppers and light pinks that swept out to the a muted gray, in which the day had begun.

That last night, I sat staring out into the far place, distances to other years and the white light of a city, much larger than in the old days.

I knew that on the stones where I was sitting the students had carved their names: Mehmet, Koray, Izmir, Ahmet, Ali, Rifat, Sinan, Hayrettin, and others; I rested, leaning on that history. I rested on that wall: gazing out.

Then from some distant minaret came a chanting voice: the last call to prayer, and then from the far East the Arabic words pierced the night, and then from the West another and another; until the blackness was filled with constant singing, a crescendo, sustained into one strong voice.

This was the sound of Turkey lifting from the Great Plains that surround the ancient city Caesarea and the gardens of Talas, echoing from the valley of Derevenk. I held my breath, black night broke.

For a moment, past time was ushered back: the darks eyes, the moments of intimacy rested down, like leaves, torn from a branch, blown out over the dusty plains in the wind, always the wind coming up.

Then slowly, the voices withdrew until there was only one and then none, and the silence came stealing in, like a peaceful death that still held my life. I left and walked down the 147 steps.

To return to a place of one's youth is to find a sacred time and place—something eventually lost to eternity.

The old buildings stood, the west wind still pressed in howls against them. The boys and young men walked in the yard, and the night wind blended with voices I had loved to hear.

In that brief time, I was once again immortal as in my youth, when I first looked out over the plains.

VIII

SPAIN

The Slide from Ibiza in the Balearic Islands of Spain

Always the film in the drawer holds the memory exact, images of the place intact.

In January, every three years, unexpectedly, I come across the slide,
hold it to the early winter night, squint in, focus on the sand, sea, and breaking wave,
quite startled to see us young again, caught unmoving, in never ending light.

We were building a sand castle; Tuson bends to lift wet sand,
Arna searches for a shell; three ships, horizon locked,
beyond my vision, in the swell of sea, gently rock.

Madame Argot, who made this island her poetry for eighty years,
sleeps in the sun to rest, while green lizards walk on the drying sand,
covering her ancient breasts.

Somewhere behind the palm trees is a basket of bread, wine, and cheese,
in a cool shadow no one sees.
I placed it there.

Quite out of distance, over the low hill, is the blue carriage and the white horse
to take us back to town,
where love stands waiting for me in the dark night,
beneath the olive trees.

Never in all these years did the head of the horse lift,
the sand fall, the shell be found, or ships sail free,
nor Madame Argot awaken to scatter the lizards to the grass,
but sleeps on in arrested sun, as if all were done.

I wonder if beneath the olive tree he waits for me,
or hears the sea breaking on pebbles and in murmurings draws back
as I hear in this night, or sees the swirling snow from his high place,
so far a distance now in years.

1982

I Gazed upon You in Your Holy Place: Dalt Villa, Ibiza, Spain

2000:

Jose Miguel Enderica Guin sings in *La Plaza de la Cruz*,
at the end of Calle Tur, where the street becomes the sea stretching to Marrakesh.

The dangerous heat of the day, the green lizards, burning scent of the pine trees,
brown grass are absorbed into the cool of the night.
I cannot turn away from the vision:
Saints' limbs dance in the wind,
and I search for the sails of great horizon ships, carrying pirates—
sweet youth on my bed in the summer of our youth;
and above all, increasing fuller,
the steadying voice of the boy from Ecuador, loudly singing Mormon hymns,
while I gaze at the fine black hair,
tussled on his legs in the sea breathing wind;
and his soft brown thighs.
We are alone in approaching dusk.

The blue ocean lifts white rolling crests
and lust becomes full in adoration
of the beauty that blossoms the rose
to an opening of sweet nectar.

"Oh, the wonder," cried St. Margaret's ascending angels in Prague,
looking back at this fair flesh;
to vision this moment, hold fast to such dark beauty.

This sacred plaza once lined with green pines—where old women in black,
crocheted white lace, whispering about neighbors, harboring great sorrows—
this place is always in my life, like a dream whose existence derives from strong
images that inflect and reflect;
no escape is possible; there is no choice;
the road is selected for me.

"And those who come into *la plaza de la cruz* are sent by God,"
says the Mormon from Guayaquil whose body is golden.
"We are bound each to each, singing of Saints, marching to the West,
not fearing the night."

Only one wave crashed against the harbored boat, secure in time.

* * *

I first sat in this park, above the sea, in 1962. *La Plaza de La Cruz* is what we called it. Now, long after the Civil War, at the end of the street, high above the sea, stood a tall wooden cross and near it was the tomb of a priest, admired by the people of Dalt Villa. That is what I saw each morning when I left the Pension of Teresa. Then I passed to the Church of Saint Dominic, and walked down to the antique shops and cafes in the town.

In the afternoon, always the same ritual. The rocks were a silently sensual place, abandoned, the staying heat forcing most to remain indoors.

In the early evening before dinner, after an afternoon of sun and diving again and again into the sea from the low cliff, the slow stopping as I sank deeper in the water, then the foaming air coming up into my ears as I slowly ascended to the surface. I would climb onto a moss covered large rock in the water and rest.

Once, when I was alone, I propped myself up on my elbows, the sharp rock pushing against me, and I watched a handsome dark soldier from the military barracks above, perhaps a gypsy, walk over to the edge of the water, facing and looking at me, he began to undress. I was mesmerized. Suddenly, two legs stood beside me. Looking up, I saw a blue and white bathing suit.

I was startled.

His voice said, "Do you like soldiers?"

I said, "I like everybody."

"Are you an American?"

"No."

We fixed a time. I would meet him in the plaza. That was the first time I saw Felipe. Our visits would continue for the next fifty-five years.

* * *

I walked up the long slope of rocks, the salt drying on my back, toward the cathedral, through the tunnel past the plaza and turned away from the sea. The fresh water shower with white ivory soap frothing all my body, took the salt away. I would be naked and clean, shivering now with the chill of night.

In dark blue shorts, a fresh white shirt which would billow in the wind, I would be conscious of my body being totally alive. The wind, the shadows, the diming light of day played on me; my body was sensual, filled with desire, as never before. The Midwest of my county, my parent's home in the country, the field of drying corn across the dusty road, the distant tower of the stern Christian Reformed Church, a startled pheasant, flying up and far out over the field, to disappear just before the woods where my kite had caught and flapped in the wind to my torment—I could free nothing I loved in that place, not even myself.

Tan, with a slight burn from three hours of swimming in the morning and two in the afternoon, I would walk out into the wind, down Calle Tur, and beyond to the plaza; the sun bleached hair on my arm raising in the cool wind up from the sea. My body was feverish with the long day in the sun, burned, lightly, I was beautiful. The kingdom of the flesh was now. I went to mass every day. My battle with God was over.

I met Felipe by the entrance to the tunnel. That day had turned dark and coolness of the night rose up. We walked among the silver olive trees, and sat down where the sea broke against the ancient cliffs. Our voices were drowned out in the screams of the cicadas. I had dreamed of such a time when I was sixteen looking out at the cornfields across the street from our small country house, listening to the crickets, suffocating with desire.

Almost every day, I would walk down to the plaza, where Madame Argot waited, with white wine and stories about D. H. Lawrence and her explanation that it was important if one wanted to write poetry, to be able to see pirate ships on the horizon.

"Now do you see them?"

"No," I said, but then squinting, I said, "Yes." It was not a lie but what I wanted to see.

Time was struck by the cathedral clock and then struck again for those who had lost their count, loud reverberating metal ringing over the sea did not signify an hour to me; it was my life, beating itself out in this place. I would live forever.

We talked about poetry and the imagination, the invention of reality—Madame Argot from France. She told me to see pirate ships on the horizon, but I could not.

You must be able to see them, or you will never be a poet. She was a great poet and a communist from France, in her eighties, crippled in a car accident in Sweden. She made much of these pirates. Their boats just on the horizon would bring lovers. I told her I could not see them.

Then squinting I said, "Yes. I see them." It was what I wanted to see.

* * *

1981:

I sat on the wall behind the Church of St. Dominic, while the wind blew strong, up the cliff from the sea, The night was mellow, a cool humidity; I was looking out at the sea, remembering my summer with Felipe and my long conversations with Madame Argot. I was choked on nostalgia, thinking of pirates; and the truth was that I could see nothing but the dark night. Images of the visit that Arna, Tuscan, Madame Argot and I made to the shore the summer of 1962: We had hired a carriage to take us to a remote beach; the carriage was blue, with a gray mare. It was a place of palm trees, green lizards, a desert heat on an island and tall grass. Arna, Tuscon, and I built a tall sand castle. I have a photo of it some place in the house. At the end of that summer, I left on the *King James II,* the same ship I had come on to Ibiza. I remembered. It had all happened so many years before. I was almost blinded by the brilliant lights illuminating the ancient Carthaginian walls, still trying to see the horizon out at sea. Some time with so many different events, people, conversations, and places, times warps and I couldn't hold on to anything. All that time had been but no longer existed. All the years blended.

Then someone was walking up toward me out of other shadows. *Arturo* stepped from beneath the pines and slowly walked toward me, a short distance. He called out to me, "Do you have a cigarette? Do you have a match?"

"Yes," I said. We talked in short sentences in Spanish. He said he was going north to be married. He wanted to make love with a man one more time.

Could he make love with me?

As we approached my hotel, he said, "Look, at the name of your hotel—*Cosario*." Pirate, I knew. I did not think of Madame Argot. I only thought of the horizon and this man who came up from the sea.

We slept in my hotel room that short night—what is it? What had happened between us?

If the voice of death had spoken, "You have had your thirst quenched in love. Now come with me," I would not have quarreled or had fear but would have surrendered like the desert reed by the river, bending down to the water.

Arturo had the fragrance of a traveler's dust. I could not take my face from his chest.

But breathed him over and over and over again.

In that soft morning light, he went north on a bus; I flew to Chicago.

2002:

Now in Ibiza, I often sit alone on the stone, my head against the iron grate,
in the same park: La Plaza de La Cruz.

In America, I look at old photographs and cannot believe the once soft beauty;
a sweet boy for men. Why, when I return, am I alone again to remember faces,
words spoken to me, and always eyes which opened all to my being. I was very
fortunate. I have only known kindness and a tender love. Some spirit broods
there for me in that plaza. It is the place of constant fresh winds. They have never
stopped blowing.
In this same wind came the Phoenicians, the Moors, the Carthaginians, and the pirates.
This is the place of the blue sea,
the soft falling of waves
over the small loose stones, against the cliff.
The sea drawing back makes the stones murmur whispered complaints,
silenced into acquisition, the drawing back.

I sat on the stone bench reading again *Brideshead Revisted*.
I wrote in my journal about the coming of the long shadows
when the sun falls down behind the cathedral
and the out islands of rock
change in just minutes from white to purple.
The wind is suddenly cool; and I feared for the moment.

I saw this young man standing by the wall, his hands on the grate;
he smiled at the sea; "So what?" I thought;
but he did not go away, still smiling and staring.
"Sonrisa," I wrote in my journal, "very strange this handsome boy staring at the sea."
I had only ten more pages to read;
and I thought I would forgo his distraction, but I turned the book over. I was drawn
into his beauty.

I myself had stood in the same spot, near the same stone, exactly as he stood. I
looked more carefully: a white T-shirt blown out in the wind, always the wind
and the brief, navy shorts, rippling jersey, revealing the outline of his body.

I looked back at the distant rocks, then turned to him again. I thought I had no
interest in him; he would leave any minute. His strong face did not move. This head
of olive complexion and his black hair were perfect; there was power, courage,
perhaps a desperate madness in the boy. I placed the book under my leg. I mused,
I said to myself, "Ah, he will never look more beautiful than he looks today. And
none shall ever see this perfection again, this moment of his great beauty and this
manliness that I see."

We were alone.

Was he looking for pirates?

Then he turned to me. "Why have you come here all this week to sit with your book
and paper? Why do you always sit here alone?"

"Well, first, I am not always alone. I often walk down here with my friends. And I
am reading and writing and having dreams."

He sat down,
first with his legs stretched out to the gravel,
but then he swung himself around quickly,
crossing his legs on the stone, like a young Buddha about to teach;

a strong wind had come up. It was cold. The wind had grown stronger, and the dark was beginning to slip in around the cathedral and rocks; we leaned toward each other to hear.

He told me he was a Mormon from Ecuador.

I looked at his legs, the fine black hair lifted up by the wind,
and the smooth olive flesh of his thighs,
warm and fragrant, I thought.

While he talked, my perception of him changed and I understood—
he was translucent, pure innocent—and I gazed at his beauty,
with a soft lust,
blown out to sea in the wind.

* * *

I write the truth now:
sometimes I say "my son,"
other times, "my brother,"
but love was never ours,
only the constant desire.

This boy from Ecuador
talked to me, corrected my Spanish,
walked around the ancient walls with me,
went to concerts with me.
He fed me a supper;
he laughed,
he teased,
he gave me his hymn book,
his New Testament,
his handkerchief,
and his jacket.

That last night, when he stood in the street behind the great house of Felipe,
I touched his face. "Que bello, que rico"; he took hold of my arm and would not let go.
I said nothing.
"Amen," the boy said as if this were the end of a supplication.

The next morning, I flew to Chicago.
The statue—saints in Santo Domingo still speak of him:
this Jose Miguel Enderico Guin, the Mormon from Ecuador.

* * *

Felipe sees him in the town a few times a year. He says he is poor.

* * *

Today I see Jose clearly, gazing out at the sea immortal in youth,
as I had stood forty years earlier. He still wears the navy shorts, the white T-shirt,
and the wind blows his black hair back. And then suddenly, he turns to me.
"Why do come here alone?"
I don't say a word.

* * *

The end of summer: 1962
        —*King James II*

On board the small white liner an American boy, with blond hair, tan face and arms, leans on the railing, looking at the Spanish lover in the shadow. The horn of the ship blows. The ropes are tossed off; the boat is free. The water churns between the boat and the dock; the distance growing wider and wider. The camera moves back and forth between the American and the Spaniard, holding the perspective of each seeing the other move away into the distance. When the ship rounds the piers in Ibiza, the boy turns from the railing and goes into the bar. He orders an absinthe. When it arrives, he walks out to the stern of the ship, where he continues to stare back at the island, but now only at the gray hills of Ibiza, and the *King James II* points away toward other land.

The next day, the young man books his passage on the SS *AKdeniz;* the ship sailed at 7:00 PM. He watched the last-minute movements on the dock, leans from the railing to see the ropes cast off. The horn blows and the ship moves away from the city of Barcelona. Later, he orders another absinthe in the bar and walks to the stern. The ship maneuvers through the long harbor and moves out into the sea. The lights of the city fade.

Then suddenly, a loud noise startles the boy. Perhaps a piece of freight fell from the top of some pile in the hold, or the ship struck a log, two logs—a shudder shook the ship, but it continued on, as if nothing had happened. The large red flag with the crescent and the star, beat wildly in the wind, snapping.

The SS *AKdeniz* steamed to sea, toward Istanbul, shuddered again with the increase of power in the pistons. He swallows some more of the drink, tastes it, and thinks for moment he has left something behind, perhaps. He is momentarily overwhelmed by doubt. He swallows more of the absinthe, tastes it. He turns away; he will live the next sixty-four years, always with these quiet doubts.

* * *

2016:

In the darkness of the sky, lovers blur into a mist of laughing faces. Voices speaking unheard words—the voices of Felipe, Arturo, and Jose are drawn back on the winds from Marrakesh.

Youth, that immortal time, went out in cold winds just above the gray rolling sea.

Rocks and High Seas

I have never really understood my life, the people with whom I have chosen to be friends, or with whom I have chosen to become intimate, sexually or on an intellectual or spiritual level, telling stories, confessing, trying to understand. I have never understood why I fell in love with Talas, a village and a school high up on a rise and ascending cliff in the interior of Turkey, or why I keep returning to Ibiza, to the olive trees along the sea, to the park at the end of Calle Pedro Tur, gazing out as if I could see the northern coast of Africa, that the riddles would suddenly open up to me and I would understand, and I would have the map, or finally accept what once was as sacred places that I might now abandon, to move beyond and live an existential life focused only on the present. But memory has been the greatest gift, and my inclination to write about it has kept me in touch with the incredible beauty of my life, despite large misfortunes.

I have never understood why I am content to pull away from social life to this strange assembly of desks pulled together, stacks of notebooks, the computer, the odd lamps, and stare out at the snow in the woods, the green leaves in the spring, house plants on my desk, sometimes fresh flowers, aware of the branches and trunks, sometimes five deer, sometimes six Turkeys, to dream, think and write. Where is it I want I want to journey, return? What understanding am I seeking? Why return again to those I felt strong akin, to celebrate love and flesh, to stir up memories and write them down?

I have never known for sure what to call these writings. The source of each is from powerful memories which return to me on almost any day that I sit in my study, looking out the window, even now in late November, the grass still green.

The memory below is of the young man I saw on the rocks, with his dog, behind the cathedral, in Ibiza, Spain. It is also about my return to see Felipe again, and our desired swim, foiled by high winds and a troubled sea. I am seventy-six; I don't expect such momentous wonders to occur again; they are a part of the time of youth and celebrate the wonder of my existence in that place, and the poignant events that have occurred for me, and the haunts. To walk again through the long lent of life, to realize before forgetting, to let pain and suffering be, not to gloss what the years have been, but to accept them, along with the joy and good fortune, coming in survival and remembrance. The joy is part of growing older, the knowing that one has lived and been conscious of the wonder of it. I don't think that when I was young I was joyful. I was, in my mind, immortal.

* * *

Journal: The Island of Ibiza, Spain; July 28, 1997:
The Foiled Swim and the Slender Youth with His Dog
Seen on the High Cliff above the Violent Sea in Ibiza

Today Felipe and I went to the rocks to swim.
What will this memory be:
gray clouds from the South had moved in?

We were surprised to see the waves high, ominous:
rounded, slow rolling swells like hills.
"No easy sliding down into the water today
on the smooth, moss-green rock,"
he said.

Below us, the sea hit against the cliff, a thud hard.
The large gray water rushing into the deep hollow ledge.
I have heard that sound only once in Spain—
the high water resisted by the hollow rock:
upward shooting, cascades,
this violent shredding of the waves,
strong enough to tear open the back of a man,
pushed deep into the recesses of the cove.

So my desire to swim once more with him, in this place, where we first had met in
1962, was undone by the Mediterranean Sea and howling wind.

He turned around and went home.
"I am going back," was all he said,
but I stayed in the chaos of the storm, fascinated,
by a writhing sea, with wind pushing me backward,
amused.

This was a dangerous place for falling and drowning;
no harness on nature sinister.
Some evil had been unleashed, broken through
like a thousand armed devils pounding on the water,
to see what was never seen before.
The salt mist blown lightly.
I laughed, a child delighted,
again salt mist on my face,
to taste on my lips.

Yes, it was there,
some cold dust from deep within the sea,
tossed up to where I sat, stung me, bitter.

Then I saw I was not alone.
A youth, some prostitute, I thought, with his small dog,
chasing a lizard: jumping, leaping, running over rocks,
The auburn color of the dog was the same as the boy's hair,
blown out in the winds, swirled against his face,
illumined for a moment, in a slice of sunlight from the parted clouds.

He stood, a slender youth, etched in my brain for all these years.
He stood trying to place a towel on the rocks in the wind.
We stared long at each other, as if daring the other,
waiting for a beckoning, some signal to come.
The other was to raise the hand or call out. Neither of us did but gazed.

The loud thud returned ominous.
I was afraid; the wind pushed our beings far apart in a roar,
or perhaps some fear and desire to know him, to hear him speak his life,
to touch his hair and share, brought fear.

After an hour, he left;
the dog zig-zagging a scent,
trotting the very edge of the high cliff.
The boy's long hair blew back
far into the winds,
and I began the long climb
up the slope of stones, scrub pine, and olive trees
to some place where the sounds and what I had seen would be no more,
knowing something lost,
a sadness in my leaving a place and remembered youth,
his and mine
to which we would not return.

IX

WAR

From a Photograph in *A Corner of a Foreign Field: Illustrated Poetry of the First World War*: Musing on the Hands of Flanders Fields

The paper, on which these poems and photographs is printed,
is thick and heavy burdened.
I think instead of turning one page, I have turned two,
and with my thumb try to separate two sides to find something in between—
that is where I want to look, to see the logic for these silenced limbs,
or see blood red poppies bloom with promise of sweeter dreams and lovers' caress,
but there is no in between to understand, or place of sane meaning,
or place to hide away.

I turn the book to see two men aright in Flanders Fields.
I want to see the faces,
but no, in death, they turned away.
The helmets slid to cover the eyes from any vision,
as if these dead could see, or know the deed done to them.

They are fresh, no bloating: the kill of early morning or of late last night's cold.
One has his right arm turned up, as if the hand would caress the thigh of the other
whose arm reaches to hold the hand resting on his flesh.
I turn the book to bring more into light the men;
I would make some tenderness of the hands,
but no, they are tossed akimbo from fallen shells.

In mud of wars, no lovers' bed exists.
I see now the arm of one is bent grotesque,
in the shell's explosion made to touch the other's thigh,
evoking no desire or tenderness.

I would separate the sides of this burdened page
to place within a gentleness,
but no, in the photograph there is no room for love I would invent,
but twisted death and each to each all wrongly bent.
Within this burdened page there is no love redeeming,
nor any space for fleeing.

2010

The Bizarre Stationary Shop

I bought a framed black-and-white postcard of twelve Jewish men
stopped at the fence of a concentration camp.
No leaves are on the trees.
Six Jews on my book case stare out at me.
The rest gaze to their right,
except for two who gaze to their left.
Three have bare hands on the barbed fence;
they stare from the iron frame that holds them;
the glass that allows them no escape—doubly confined, holds my reflection peering in.
They look at me as if they have asked a question and are waiting for the answer.
Or I have asked the question and they are silent with me;
what words could hold their answer?

I notice two handsome men: the one in the front with his hand on his chin,
and the other in the second row, almost in the center;
his eyes a sensual darkness, deep set in shallow hollows.
In the dusk of this night, white plumes like the feathers of a phoenix,
an incense drawn up, to lift and free them.

I am haunted into these old photographs of Jews in concentration camps.
Into this one, out in the yard at night I intrude, searching for handsome men,
like the one in the center with his lower lip turned slightly out—
and my love making would not be selfish, only to pleasure him,
to lie in bed until in warmth he dreamed of his blue bike,
riding far from home into the white haze of spring; or my soul, if he wished, I would
give to him.

In the upper-left corner, someone has pasted a postage stamp:
Hitler gazing into a mirror, just beyond the margin of the photograph.

All will turn away to some graveyard in my brain,
but not this one with his lower lip turned out, he remains,
and in one step is up against the fence.
He stares at me, not knowing white blossoms of spring opening,
nor to rise like the Phoenix from his ashes.
He stares at me until I turn away, swallowed by enigma:
beauty once alive.

1998

From a Great Distance Falling

One November, while driving with two friends along the icy roads
of an early Michigan winter,
looking for antique shops: a pedestal is what I wanted,
old, for an abundant green fern,
but the day lost meaning.
We passed cornfields with a light snow marking the rows of stubble,
among the clods of frozen dirt;
and a strange sorrow came falling from far away:
I said, "Let's tell a story from childhood."

"The boy who taught me how to tie my shoes,
a pilot in WWII, was shot down over the Pacific.
As a boy I saw him once upon his bed,
sleeping naked in the morning sun,
gleaming his blond hair and flesh to gold,
like a God, from an ancient time,
returned in soft splendor on which to gaze out dreams,
a mysterious love of
such perfection, a radiant beauty came into me.

My mother later explained
why he would not return;
and I saw and heard,
the plane like an arc
from a great distance falling,
white in smoke against the blue sky,
into a darker sea."

Ours was a cold month:
a hard time to remember the innocence of such vision;
his beauty gone these long years,
never to be looked upon,
nor worshiped again,
brought low in the sea,
far from the sun and his warm bed,
to the chill of invisible currents.

2004

The Victory of the Handsome
Iraqi Man: The News Online

The rage of your handsome face,
made by the sun and wind, strong tanned.
I remember your head covered.

Before you spoke,
I saw you, the utter sheer beauty of your eyes,
the perfect flesh of your face: black mustache and beard;

As I looked up to the screen, while mending the fringe on a Turkish rug.
I was astonished to see you standing there, clutching your bags of rice and flour,
your bottles of clean water—
all tossed out upon you, not given—the box thrown hard.
You lost your balance, wrestled low to keep it, but righted up, intact,
and humiliation flamed to rage, thus to receive poisoning sustenance,
the blood in the raised veins of your neck, pulsating.

And the dusty blond journalist to make a story said in his never-ending
battery of questions: "What do you think of Americans?"

I marveled:
the convulsion of anger tore through your body to your face and lips to kill,
"I hate American, I hate British."

I marveled: so perfect a humiliation forcing your blade-sharp dignity
to consume the vile souls who devoured your land,
then fed you,
as farm boys to pigs.

2003

Death in Iraq: A Rushing in of Spring

Here, this rush in of red geraniums, firm in terra-cotta pots,
the unfurling daily of green, and more shaded skeins
from maple, oak, black locus;
and primal fern, uncurling—
all is a wave of strength, born against the winter, hard it pushes up,
lifting creation's act as in eons of time.
Now this simplest fragrance of purple petunia, velvet spice.
Sun-shadowed scent is all the season's reconciliation.
The harmony of design making life the new season,
seen in a green wicker chair, with tea, toast and honey.

Far from me, fire shells are shot hot to the faces of children,
unwittingly, of course; why not?
It was the brown eyed man they meant,
but still, the children felt the hate, like salt and acid melting.

Here in Iowa, the mother shaking water and white suds
above a kitchen sink does not hear,
in that single moment, all gather to put him down, the son,
who now knows the sure aim of a gun,
shot from across the road;
the same son now she dreams a boy with his first bike,
both jerking and wobbling,
until he fell down, down,
while she gazes at promises of lilac lace:
a shawl to cover far away a melting face.
blood, fire-white hot
and mute the scream of steel fast shot
to the silence of a man.

In this minute, in spring: a flame, a single metal lance,
the gentle nodding branch,
the clean spice scent of a purple flower,
tea, toast, and honey,
here in my safe green wicker chair.

The distance among them is thousands of miles
and a bitter irony.

2010

Looking at a Postcard of Jews Lined Against a Fence in 1944

My Jewish lover, dead,
in dreams and afternoon prayers
returns to haunt from his time in April, near the fence,
to this winter, cold in remembrance
of him,
black hair, gaunt
his sorrow eyes,
stares through wires at me,
beyond the beginning of spring,
to a single branch of white buds promising
a coming from deep within the earth to flower,
a fragrance cascading,
fair, tender-lipped,
he searches for the living, the moving, the opening;
like a cat distracted, his vision darts around his small earth.

My brother,
kin, red blood, merged in desire—
and German ancestor,
devoured in white flames;
I remember the softness of your mouth
opened to the spring wind-cool,
your arms in no shadow
beneath the clouded sun.

From the black stacks,
never-ending;
ascending, spirit deities who desired flesh,
Yahweh called man to love man, vanish.

* * *

In the room once, now long left behind,
the youth (I could not have been more), once stirring in dreams
called out his name,
while petals, never seen,
fell just beneath the wind.

I cannot know his thoughts,
who looking at the woods where he would never be,
sees something in the trees
or just beyond;
hears a voice call out,
or hears the bird,
or falling branch,
on this last day,
and tries to make meaning to himself;
but cannot rise above the simple scent of spring
from deep inside the woods
and some almost forgotten thing
he loved
in ancient youth.

So I vision
into this man
of ashen petals,
still alive,
against the fence.

1980

The Importance of Linear
Perspective in Photography

With my magnifying glass, I see this photograph is of small pieces: the rafters of
a roof—the tiles shelled away.
Wooden supports lean together like the fine white bones of a fish decaying on
a beach.
I would say fifty-three wooden beams collapsed together;
counted with the metal point of my ruler.
A long fence angles straight back to the distant wall,
rows of poles lean left, askew, and right.
Although it is broken, the fence seems sturdy, confining all within itself,
narrowing to a distant gate, unhinged, stuck . . . nothing beyond.

This linear study is viewed from above; the photographer is not in the place.

The picture is perfect stasis—nothing moves within this place,
except for American soldiers, with misfortune to be sent there—form lines at right
angles.
I, looking carefully through the magnifying glass, can see their legs in walking
patterns,
interrupted by the click of the shutter.

The photograph contains a silence,
like a vacuum to draw us in.
Let no one out, beyond the fallen wall,
the gate heavy off hinges,
still closed, nothing beyond.

In the foreground are six bodies the size of my small finger;
we can see the eye sockets, but the skin is pulled too tight,
so there are no lips to kiss, no mouth to scream,
arms twisted, feet to the left; legs unnaturally folded.
In the far distance, the bodies are the size of my fingernail
and look like heaps of clothes.

I turn the photograph around and the narrowed linear opens like a parted sea:
the faces upside down,
the chest and buttocks confused.
these men already drowned.

With the glass, I look for some handsome youth, a familiar face, there is none I know.
One voice slides into the silence from the other side;
naked Isaiah sings of the Messiah, but no eyes saw such sweet promise fulfilled, nor I.

The focus isn't right;
the glass too far from the event.

2009

Shiloh*

I am told the handsome face becomes a skull;
and pigs feed on flesh a woman kissed—the hands of this farm boy,
when once roused in sweet scent of hay.

A country church named the battle: Shiloh, to speak aloud,
with the beauty of sound like Shenandoah—only Shiloh, to speak aloud.
Shiloh—what harm could come to a place so named: Peace, with a vast green field
and acres of peach trees in bloom?

Stray bullets struck the trees, branches, and blossoms,
Petals, as if strewn for a wedding bed, dropped ceaselessly on the thousand dead.
Each man having seen the face of each man he killed,
a frenzied hornets' next for half a day, he said—
this ancient energy, blood and hate, heated on by the sight of blue or gray,
in the scent of the other man's sweat.

Night fell dark; all sound was silenced.
Soldiers beaten with weariness dropped down among the dead to sleep.
Lighting and thunder replaced cannon and rifle—
the pummel of rain, as if Divinity would cleanse the crime illumined:
The dead and weary, brothers in rest that last night,
while the cloud misted moon descended in small light.

Among the sleeping and slain, soft words drifted—
the boy in gray speaking to a photograph:
a young woman, as if she came for him in this long time of his bleeding,
to hear again his pledge of love.

Slow-dying soldiers often gaze at gossamer images
and whisper, so not to die alone.

2008

---

*   Concept source: Civil War Trilogy, Shelby Foote

The Battle of Malvern Hill*

I see in these hot days of July, leaping images;
Civil War netted in a shroud of words.
No present time, but sit each day and night in darkness of another time,
seduced to fear and grief by lurid detail in McPherson's book.

I read to those earlier days to become voyeur of men's foul intimacies:
arms lifted to the other, misshaped embraces,
a hand holding soft the other's face,
and hand to hand;
their passionate proximities in death to each other on native land.
And remember the running soldier's terror,
the sighing of the final bullet marked for him;
for a short moment, he continued running: a bolting corpse,
then collapsed, never to gain again such delicate balance.

This is a hill for fallen men, who give exhausted cries to wounds:
the speaking flesh of a severed leg, a throat pierced but still voicing out in fog
to protest such violation, to surrender dreams of their fathers' fields in summer and
tender love of a woman who beckons to her arms.

Morning light burns the pall of fog,
a veil to conceal no longer all the open, wide field stretched to far distance,
the catafalque slanted by the woods: shrub, green fern and undergrowth,
the overspreading on a hill of wild grass, milkweed, and Queen Anne's lace:
to show the living, scarce living, and the bloated dead, rising from all—a sour
breath.

Then see those thousands wounded, with only strength enough to creep,
to slither on bellies, to drag on hands and feet as dogs,
as if the hill itself would crawl away from this charnel place;
and escape the baptism of such auspicious blood.

2009

---

*   Concept source: Civil War Series, Shelby Foote

X

RANDOM WRITINGS

Lovers in My Tabernacle Dwell

Inside my window, white-petaled cyclamen dance—danseurs against the winter glass.
Snow falls light, drifting sideways in lake wind.
Red Hawthorne berries knock against the bricks,
hanging for spring and bird beaks.

Inside this room of icons and books, photographs of ancestors,
candle wicks burn and incense, slow twirls up a warmth—
all a tabernacle makes strong against evil and the dark—
those who understand Christ in fear and hate.

* * *

But I confess my loves:

Felipe the Spaniard:

I remember my lovers on the island of Ibiza through all my life,
an isolated place of passions.
the SS *King James II* glided me there through rain;
the shores appeared in mist.
I was twenty-two.

The day came when Felipe stood near me on the rocks.
The sea drew in and out,
sounding a small breaking wave on pebbles, pulled suddenly back.

That night, beneath pungent olive blossoms, among the sage,
high on the cliff we knew our freedom
in that scent and sound.

I sing this room, a tabernacle of holiness and good fortune.
At summer's end, he asked me to stay.
I had to return to Istanbul, and said no.

Two days later, after sunset and I was leaning on the varnished wood—
the railing of the SS *AKdeniz*; the day clouded over,
the lights of Barcelona vanished in the taste of raki sweet on my tongue;

and at that moment, a chunk of wood or a trunk fell below.
In that minute of fear,
I had doubted all I was and had said.

* * *

Koray the Turk:

In this room, a tabernacle, of incense, the scent of manly beauty recollected,
pens and paper, while snow never stopping, rises up,
caught in the swirling dry wind above the Anatolian plains
where Basil the Great of Caesarea and Gregory of Nazianzen,
revealed heavenly mysteries, created creeds that speak today,
I saw lean youth revealed to me
with raven hair, dark eyes
step out of line and stare at me.
I never spoke to him that year, nor he to me.

But later at Tarsus he asked me if I would go swimming with him and some others
at the beach near Mersin, where a river empties into the Mediterranean Sea.
After crossing the river among reeds, the barge lodged.
We came to the white sand and water the sea stretching to Cairo.

The others went to a café. We talked about Edward Albee, Andre Gide—
the books we read, the lean youth's art—
his paintings I saw upstairs one dark night in Tarsus—some male erotic.
He was playful, intelligent, and beautiful—a time of intimate desire.
But I would never know him as I desired,
only to desire him all my life.

Death to him came too soon—twenty-two, in Ankara. One shot.

The gardens come again from that high place in Talas:
red poppies, blue iris, and the tree in flowers
like white late summer moths to flutter distance away.

* * *

Christ the Jew:

He all wonder holds of creation and passion—
word made flesh entwined, cosmic beyond us,
washing dusty feet; his body given to waiting lips.

Lovers in my tabernacle dwell.
Here it is the icon that stands in perfection,
a singing image of richest being and mysterious loss,
slipping away in time,
even my own oblivion.

Lovers in my tabernacle,
still dwell,
beneath sure Pentecostal flame, a light against all darkness;
and a rushing of wind,
*if only I let it bear me, carry me, if only it carry me!**

2015

---

*   *Song of the Man Who Comes Through* – D. H. Lawrence

A Vestry Devotion on a Stained Glass Window, Christ the King: St. Mark's Episcopal Church, Grand Rapids, Michigan in 1981

Outside this window is an alley;
across the cobblestones, a college;
to the West, a museum;
this center stretches to suburbs, farm land,
a great lake, and world.

Within this window is space where sound of traffic enters, the siren of suffering,
where the poor have sat with one bag of possessions,
and the people receive Him,
each journeying up and back on a creaking floor,
echoing footfalls,
echoing some other time.

Beneath this window is an altar, a screen,
a brass cross, molded metal to a brilliance, reflecting light,
where kneeling with my kin, the incense lifting all of me into deep blue mysteries
of Mary
and the red blood glass of Christ the King who has for years been here,
each time companion, when I have entered in;
on days of brightest sun,
light making holy kaleidoscope on my hand, lifted to receive Him
who redeems over and again,
Lover of my body and soul,
who will not let me go.

This dark wooded place, of pews, beams, screens,
and the richest brown of altar,
waxed, sheening salvation,
where Christ is lifted from his tomb, how many times?
Where those who watch, grieve to comfort, how many times?
Where those who fail, confess;
who sink in emptiness, hold hand to be filled with sacred flesh;
where outcast dares walk in;
where Christ, with all saints, even my dead, has come to me,
how many times?

This place of sacred beauty,
made by ancestors, bringing river stones on carts,
the towers rising up, placing the icon windows, which speak in day and night, the
stations of the cross to sign the tragedies of humanity and perfection for human
bond rejected, killing truth and compassion—
ancestors, who like us, could not measure then this now and future,
the redemption and love poured out to the numberless who were taught here,
for their darkest night,
to survive somehow with each other,
clinging to old words,
the ancient lifting up,
and our singing here—
them, now dead,
us, alive a day,
and those to come—
make praise
against chaos,
make joy to us, to them, to him.

May this house always be,
and bring surging song against the dirge,
to bring union for those separated,
to say, "Our Christ the King is kindest of all shepherds,
who cares for each and brings love,
each to each,
none ever turned away,
but taught to be as him;
to know the burden, light and yoke, not heavy."

That beneath this window—
        where sun passes through purple,
        bell rings out steady across the river,
        organ and choir sound in psalms,
        sermon speaks,
        bread and wine offered,
        while candles flicker on the even stitches of the altar cloth—precise;
        and words, for centuries spoken against all odds—precise,
        bring Son in sun:
        "This is my Body, my Blood";
        and all soars up,
        to splinter down again,

penetrating heavy doubt,
the mystery broken and made more,
in breathless awe,
spilling from the fonts
of the white lamb,
sweetest love—
all breathe in the wind of Holy Ghost wings beating,
beating to rest in us the seed of Christ—
and we say,
"Yes."

We know our home is him—the Shepherd King still wounded;
within this window and outside these ancient stones,
made from a melting ice—
one more day,
a living house;
from cosmic dawn,
a light against the darkness, a rushing wind.

1981